HOW TO TRANSFORM
STRATEGIC INITIATIVES INTO
BLOCKBUSTER RESULTS

Implementation

ALAN P. BRACHE
SAM BODLEY-SCOTT

McGraw-Hill

New York   Chicago   San Francisco   Lisbon   London   Madrid   Mexico City
Milan   New Delhi   San Juan   Seoul   Singapore   Sydney   Toronto

This publication is designed to provide accurate and authoritative information in regard to the subject matter covered. It is sold with the understanding that the publisher is not engaged in rendering legal, accounting, or other professional service. If legal advice or other expert assistance is required, the services of a competent professional person should be sought.
    —*From a declaration of principles jointly adopted by a committee of the American Bar Association and a committee of publishers.*

McGraw-Hill books are available at special quantity discounts to use as premiums and sales promotions, or for use in corporate training programs. For more information, please write to the Director of Special Sales, McGraw-Hill Professional, Two Penn Plaza, New York, NY 10121-2298. Or contact your local bookstore.

 This book is printed on recycled, acid-free paper containing a minimum of 50% recycled, de-inked fiber.

Microsoft Project and Microsoft Project Central are registered trademarks.

Contents

Foreword

FOR ANYONE WHO IS RESPONSIBLE for a results-driven organization, this book is going to be a good—and useful—read.

A recent article in *Harvard Business Review* (Thomas Davenport, "The Coming Commoditization of Processes," June 2005) reported on the trend toward outsourcing as the preferred method of "process improvement." Davenport refers to the ever-present, nearly universal desire of organizational leaders to improve the way they do business.

Indeed, business-process improvement has been much in vogue over the past decade and is a popular subject for good reason. In today's competitive environment, it is essential that an organization "develop muscle" to deal with rapidly changing conditions: markets, competition, technology, supply chain, governmental and regulatory intervention, economic conditions, and an ability to source capital that often changes by the hour.

Clearly, an organization that has a deep understanding of these environmental conditions, that has clearly defined its strategic intent, and that is aligned under committed, inspired leadership has an edge on the competition. An organization that also has a demonstrated ability to implement its strategy successfully while controlling the number of initiatives it undertakes—and thereby tying up only a portion of its resources—is one to be reckoned with.

Using a disciplined process to identify, set priority on, and tackle strategic initiatives does not come naturally to most business leaders. Even smart, experienced, dedicated leaders have a tendency to take a heads-down, task-oriented, fragmented, and reactionary approach to this exercise. The application of a rigorous, systematic approach such as the one outlined in *Implementation* is a learned behavior—one that is definitely worth investing the time to master.

In today's fast-paced business world, where we're often looking for quick results, it is easy to fall prey to the "let's do something now" mentality. Confident, successful leaders are often certain that they know what's best for the business. Without a well-formulated, well-communicated strategy, managers at all levels of the organization use their clout and resources to push their pet projects through the system. Ideas and activities spring up from all corners faster than they can be identified—much less controlled. Completely unrelated to the organization's priorities, these uncontrolled, unapproved, sometimes even undiscovered activities sap organizational time, money, and energy that are desperately needed elsewhere.

At best, the failure to commit to a strong process for strategic planning and the implementation of initiatives to support this strategy results in inefficiency. At worst, it could cause an organization to fail. Clearly, a well-understood, cohesive strategy executed with a limited number of meaningful initiatives is a better alternative—avoiding as it does frustration, confusion, and the erosion of customer satisfaction, sales, and profits.

Alan Brache and Sam Bodley-Scott define strategy as "the framework of choices that determines the nature and direction of an organization" or, more succinctly, as "the water in which you swim." Although *Implementation* is not focused on the construction of strong business strategy, that task is the fundamental precursor to initiative development. One will not work without the other. Strategy only points you in a direction; it is implementation, through strategic initiatives, that provides the forward movement.

The value of *Implementation* is that it introduces a framework—the disciplined process so often lacking—for the implementation of strategy. When mastered, the principles that the book introduces are bound to prevent many of the organizational lapses or oversights that often hamstring strategic change. Following these basic principles will encourage alignment, create focus and efficient utilization of resources, and enable evolution of a brand or business.

Implementation focuses on the identification, prioritization, and management of those critical few initiatives that derive from strategy and, as such, lead to competitive advantage. Alan and Sam have organized a structured, step-by-step approach to one of the most challenging of organizational "essential functions": *managing change in a purposeful direction with limited resources.*

The success of an organization comes down, in the end, to leadership. *Implementation* is written from the perspective of executive leadership. Regardless of the size of your organization, if you are responsible for providing the leadership required to "carry the day," at the end of that day it won't be the documents you produce, the meetings you chair, or the good intentions you express that count. It will be the *results* you achieve. This book will help you deliver those results.

Cy Taylor
President and Chief Operating Officer
Cracker Barrel Old Country Store, Inc.

Acknowledgments

OUR THANKS TO:

Our clients, who partnered with us on their strategy implementation journey and provided us with opportunities to test and refine the ideas, tools, and processes presented in this book. We would especially like to thank Cy Taylor from Cracker Barrel, Linda Hudson from General Dynamics, Stacy Brovitz from Dormont Manufacturing, Simon Brocket from Coca-Cola Enterprises, Abdelgadir Khalil from DAL Group, John Flanagan from EBS Building Society, Andy Cook from Fujifilm Electronic Imaging, and Annette Flynn from United Drug.

The members of "The Bull, Streatley" review panel, whose thoughtful feedback helped us shape and position our arguments.

Bruce Keener, Kepner-Tregoe CEO, who sponsored this book project.

Our colleagues at Kepner-Tregoe, who provided feedback on the draft manuscript. Particular thanks to Andrew Longman for his pinpointed, balanced, constructive critique.

Judie Morello, who provided first-class, quick turnaround document support.

Peter Tobia and Dale Corey, our literary agents from Market Access, who helped us pinpoint the message and refine its expression.

Jeanne Glasser, our McGraw-Hill editor, who championed the project, provided feedback on our first draft, and led the process that brought this book to fruition.

Manda, Jack, and Harry Bodley-Scott, who had to play second fiddle during the writing of this book.

Alan Brache
Sam Bodley-Scott

STRATEGY IMPLEMENTATION:

The Responsibility That Makes or Breaks Executives

*P*HILIP BORDEN, THE CEO OF HAMMERSMITH INDUSTRIES, *a $500 million designer and manufacturer of semiconductor fabrication equipment,[1] is facing formidable strategic challenges. As a result of heightened geopolitical tension in both the Middle East and Asia, the global economy is uncertain. Consumer demand for personal computers has weakened. Competition from the Taiwanese is increasingly formidable. U.S. corporate and government IT spending continues to be weak and price-driven.*

In addition to these external pressures, Philip is wrestling with equally daunting strategic challenges from inside Hammersmith. During its annual strategy review, the executive team decided that the company's future success would revolve around two competitive advantages that the company does not currently possess: the ability to customize equipment to meet unique customer needs and the quality and speed of its customer service.

Philip isn't intimidated by changing market conditions or increased competition; he is paid to tackle issues in those areas. Nor is he having second thoughts about his team's bet-the-ranch strategic decisions. However, he is frustrated with the quality and pace of implementation. In the six months since the review, he has seen little progress in developing and installing the processes that will operationalize the company's chosen competitive advantages.

He has attempted to identify the causes of the lack of results. He doesn't think it's the viability of the vision; it was forged with considerable deliberation and founded on exhaustive research. He doesn't think it's lack of understanding; he has consistently and simply communicated the vision and has established clear direction to those responsible for aligning the business with that vision. Whenever he interacts with someone—at any level—he tests that person's grasp of the "what" and "why" of the strategy. He is consistently satisfied with the answers he gets.

His most talented resources cannot say that they are unable to pursue strategic issues because they are overly consumed with day-to-day operations; he has relieved them of as many tactical duties as is possible without compromising sales, manufacturing, and delivery. And it's not a money issue; Philip has agreed to every funding request needed to support strategy implementation, including some for which the business case is not as complete or as compelling as he would like.

Philip sees lots of "molecules in motion" around strategy implementation. People at all levels can frequently be found in conference rooms with flip-chart pages taped to the walls, facilitators wielding markers and clicking through PowerPoint slides, and steam coming from their heads. However, while there's lots of activity, the results are agonizingly slow in coming. When Philip requests a progress report, people scurry to get him status information. When he asks when milestones will be reached, they waffle.

He doesn't understand the genesis of many of the current ini-tiatives that are being pursued under the strategy implementation banner. While each of them appears to have a noble intent, he does-n't see how they are going to contribute to the deployment of his vision.

He doesn't know the amount of resources being consumed by these efforts, but he is sure that having time and money informa-tion would frustrate him even further.

Philip's angst level would be significantly lower if he thought that one or more of his executives had a firmer grip on the situa-tion than he does. They don't. While his colleagues share his vision and his perception that progress has been slow, each of them sees only a part of the "strategy implementation" picture; nobody appears to have the entire vista in his or her sights.

Philip thinks he has the talent he needs, but he doesn't think that people are appropriately focused on the company's most impor-tant pursuit. He realizes that even a compelling vision does not become reality without the coordinated deployment of a manage-able set of well-run initiatives. While he knows that a "just do it" directive from him won't get the job done, he's not sure what will.

THE CHALLENGE OF STRATEGY IMPLEMENTATION

Philip and his team may or may not have a vision that will ensure Hammersmith's success in the future. However, the odds are that he'll never know. Without a disciplined process for driving strategy from the boardroom to the back office, it is difficult, if not impossible, to measure success. The number of bad strategies that are well implemented is dwarfed by the number of good strategies that are poorly implemented. Con-sider the following:

*   Former Sony CEO Nobuyuki Idei was among the first executives to see the potential in the convergence of media and electronics. He forged a vision of a Sony that would offer an entertainment package containing both

content and the hardware for its delivery. Maybe it was the wrong strategy, but we will never know, because Idei was not able to put into place the processes and structure to implement it. Concerns over piracy slowed down development. In spite of having a leg up with its Walkman, Sony was blindsided by Apple's iPod. Idei couldn't get agreement on technical standards or a pricing model. He wasn't able to align the company across countries and functional "silos." While Sony excelled in its gaming business, it was not able, under Idei's leadership, to master an integrated and compelling set of movie/music/electronics offerings.[2]

- Many have criticized former Hewlett-Packard CEO Carly Fiorina's strategy of integrating HP's product lines and establishing a more formidable presence in the personal computer business through the purchase of Compaq. As in the case of Sony, we'll never know whether her vision was viable because it was never realized. Famously imperial and hands off, she never meshed with the deep-rooted culture (the "HP way"). She failed to communicate the what/why/how of her strategy effectively and to build the commitment of the people who were critical to its implementation. Strategic accomplishment was not built into expectations, measures, rewards, and feedback.[3]

- Lynne Camp, the vice president and general manager of Agilent Technologies' Systems Generation and Delivery Unit, wanted to forge a single global company. Few people questioned the degree to which accomplishing that goal would create a strong competitive advantage. However, that vision crumbled under the weight of interfunctional squabbles, slow executive decision making (out of fear of taking their eyes off their ongoing responsibilities), failure to involve the "best and the brightest" in strategy implementation, and communication that was limited to behind-closed-doors sessions.[4]

- The European Union created the "Lisbon strategy," which established an ambitious mission: building the most competitive economy in the world by instituting business-friendly policies that would invigorate the economies of all countries. That lofty goal was not achieved because it died of asphyxiation after its translation into 28 "objectives," 120 "targets," and 117 "indicators." Each member state was distracted, if not paralyzed, by having to produce 300 reports. It's not too late for Europe to establish itself as the dominant global economy; however, if it does, it will be because it has now defined a narrower and more achievable focus on services and employment.[5]

You have a personal stake in this pursuit. Leadership experts estimate that 70 percent of CEOs who fail are ineffective not because their vision is flawed, but because they are unable to implement that vision.[6] Not surprisingly, "execution" has become a mantra on mahogany row.

WHAT IS STRATEGY?

Before we double-click on strategy implementation, we should be clear as to what we mean by strategy. We define strategy as *the framework of choices that determines the nature and direction of an organization*. Strategy is a *framework* because it should serve as the context for all activities; it should be the water in which you swim. It is about tough *choices*—will do/won't do lines in the sand—not about lofty platitudes that provide little guidance. It does not include the multitude of day-to-day choices that are made in any organization; it encompasses only the small number of seminal product, market, and competitive decisions that determine what the organization is (*nature*) and where it is going (*direction*).

There is only one reason to establish a strategy: to focus investment. If you commanded infinite resources, you wouldn't need a strategy; you'd simply throw a steady stream of products and services at the market wall and see what sticks. A strategy says, "We have finite financial resources, and here is where we're going to spend our hard-earned money. We have finite human resources, and here is where we're going to dedicate the precious time of our talented people."

Specifically, a strategy answers these questions:

- How far down the road will we look?

- Based on the most up-to-date intelligence, what are our assumptions about the market, the competition, regulation, the economy, and other factors in our external environment?

- What are our fundamental values and beliefs?

- What products or services will we and will we not offer during this time horizon?

- What markets will we and will we not serve during this time horizon?

- Which products or services and markets will receive the greatest emphasis?

- What are our competitive advantages (i.e., how will we win)?

- What capabilities (skills, processes, facilities, and equipment) will we need to fulfill this vision?

- What financial and nonfinancial measures will we use to assess our strategic performance?

Your organization may not have addressed these questions. Or the answers may not be viable, specific, compelling, up to date, or consistently understood and passionately supported by your executive team. However, closing that gap is not the focus of this book.[7] We are addressing a question that is less glamorous but at least as consequential and typically more difficult: How can we transform our vision into reality?

THE COMPONENTS OF STRATEGY IMPLEMENTATION

The Enterprise Model[8] depicted in Figure 1-1 was created to provide executives with a holistic picture of all the variables

FIGURE 1-1 The Enterprise Model

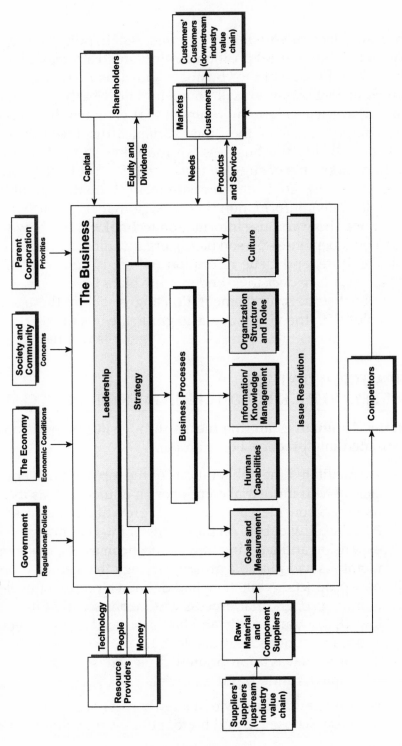

that influence an organization's success. It puts "strategy" squarely in the central position. A pinpointed strategy defines the size and shape of the "business" box (the market space in which an organization will compete) and clearly articulates how it will win in an environment that contains the market, the competition, and the other variables displayed around that box. Inside the business, surrounding strategy, are the eight components of strategy *implementation*: leadership, business processes, goals and measurement, human capabilities (people skills), information/knowledge management (which is not only how you use information technology, but how you learn on a person-to-person basis), organization structure and roles, culture, and issue resolution (which is how you solve problems, make decisions, and execute plans).

Robust strategy implementation aligns each of these eight variables with the vision that is to guide the business.

STRATEGIC INITIATIVES: THE KEYS TO THE KINGDOM OF IMPLEMENTATION SUCCESS

Strategic initiatives are the means through which a vision is translated into practice. For example,

- We facilitated the deliberations of the top team of a small, closely held industrial component manufacturer as its members considered a number of growth alternatives. After healthy debate on the merits of international expansion and entering new domestic markets, the team members had forged a growth strategy that centered on new products. While they had defined a product development process, that process was inconsistently followed, slow, and costly and had produced few winners. The team launched a strategic initiative to ensure that this process was appropriately designed, staffed, IT-enabled, funded, and followed.

- We guided the strategy of a large consumer products company whose top and bottom lines were being eroded by Asian imports that were equivalent in quality and lower in price. After evaluating and rejecting a number of alternative paths out of this thicket, the top team made two strategic decisions: to partner with a small set of Chinese manufacturers, and to establish order-fulfillment cycle time as a competitive advantage. The team commissioned initiatives to achieve each of these strategic intents.

- We helped the executives of a defense contractor's business unit identify and evaluate the capabilities that were critical to the unit's competitive success and profitability. During that exercise, the executive team identified supply-chain management (SCM) as a deficiency that not only generated internal frustration but actually constituted a competitive disadvantage. The team invested heavily in a strategic initiative to install leadership, processes, and systems that would give the unit competitive parity in SCM as it pursued advantages in other areas.

Without successful initiatives, strategy implementation is impossible. Acquisitions can't be made. New products can't be created and commercialized. New markets can't be entered. Competitive advantages can't be forged and maintained. Brand equity can't be established or enhanced. Costs can't be driven out of a supply chain. Talent can't be developed.

In most cases, the most pivotal strategic need is to create and sustain—for as long as possible in a fast-changing world—a competitive advantage. For example, we helped a European mobile telecommunications company formulate and implement its corporate strategy. As a result of consolidation in that industry, the network and systems infrastructure of a number of providers had become a complex amalgam of different legacy systems that were difficult to configure in a way that supported new services and tariffs. During their strategy formulation, the company's executives realized that they could establish a powerful competitive edge by reducing the time it takes to replace legacy systems with a new, integrated technology platform that was capable of responding flexibly to market needs. They launched an initiative to create a process for rapidly converting or replacing such systems as new technologies emerge.

The speedy and successful implementation of this strategic initiative created a 12-month window during which the company introduced a range of mobile services and tariffs that customers perceived as clearly superior to those offered by competitors, who were still encumbered with old technology. Because the initiative produced a process, not just a one-time effort, the company retained the substantial gains in market share that were achieved during the initial implementation period.

SEIZING THE UNKNOWN

The strategy implementation challenge is particularly daunting when incremental change will not take you to where you must go. Perhaps your market's needs (e.g., its expectations for service) or buying criteria (e.g., price sensitivity) are significantly different from what they were in the past. Or perhaps the competitive landscape has been dramatically altered (e.g., consolidation into a small number of major players or the appearance of formidable offshore suppliers). Practical application of nanotechnology may be leapfrogging your current systems. Or the regulatory environment may have become increasingly tight, given a shifting political climate. In such cases, a mere midcourse correction to your strategy may simply prolong the agony.

Entering a "brave new world" puts an increased demand on the change management dimension of your leadership responsibilities. As Kevin Kelly put it, "The new rules governing . . . global restructuring revolve around several axes. First, wealth in this new regime flows directly from innovation, not optimization; that is, wealth is not gained by perfecting the known, but by imperfectly seizing the unknown."[9]

Strategic initiatives are your vehicles for seizing the unknown.

DO YOU KNOW WHERE YOU STAND?

As you deploy strategic initiatives, the odds are stacked against your success. Research on strategic initiatives involving the installation of new information technology[10] has shown that only 28 percent meet their goals on time and within budget. Another 18 percent are canceled. The remaining 54 percent limp to the finish line with objectives compromised and/or significant overruns relative to time and budget projections. Earlier research[11] indicates that the average initiative goes 89 percent over budget and takes 122 percent longer than planned.

Is your organization's performance significantly better than these bleak numbers? If not, can you afford the luxury of this level of ineffectiveness? And potentially more disturbing: Do you know how much you are investing in strategic initiatives and what the return on that investment is?

For example, a large information technology infrastructure company's top team took a deep breath and forged a high-risk strategy. They decided to exit the businesses that had served as the bedrock on which the company had been built. To fill the gap, they invested a significant amount of their future success in the rapid introduction of successful new products. It was a bold but dicey move, given this organization's lackluster track record of product commercialization. We asked the vice president of product development to provide an estimate of the current level of activity. His answer: "Our pipeline contains 25 to 30 product development projects." Our subsequent analysis revealed quite a different story. Much to the surprise of the vice president, we discovered more than 200 products in various stages of development. While most of these projects were not getting much attention, all of them were getting some level of effort, thereby siphoning focus from the "critical few."

If you are a typical senior executive—especially the CFO— you undoubtedly know the cost of ongoing operations. Chances are that you have headcount and productivity metrics that can easily be translated into dollars. And we would be surprised if these numbers were not reported regularly. But ask yourself this: "Is our performance against initiatives regularly monitored, reported, and used as the basis for our decision making?" If not, shouldn't your progress toward the deployment of your strategy be prominently displayed on your radar screen?

KILLERS OF STRATEGY IMPLEMENTATION

We are frequently asked to audit an organization's strategy implementation. We have found that one of the hallmarks of best-in-class companies and agencies is the role played by their executives. You are responsible for creating the infrastructure, climate, and processes in which initiatives produce change. One of your pivotal roles is to see that action is taken to avoid the eight booby traps that typically derail strategy implementation:

1. FAILING TO LAUNCH THE RIGHT INITIATIVES

It's easy to fall into this trap if you have a strategy that doesn't fully answer the questions in our "what is strategy?" discussion. This failure may also be due to not knowing what needs to be done to execute some key element of the strategy: "We need to establish service after the sale as a competitive advantage. How do we do that?" In addition, resource-sapping, nonstrategic initiatives may be launched without executives being aware of them. You may set people off on the wrong path as a result of insufficiently specific communication. ("Are we entering the China market or merely evaluating its potential?" "Are we changing our brand or merely testing it in a new market?" "Are we setting out to transform the industry or merely to improve our performance in the industry as currently defined?")

If you are clearly communicating the "what," is the "why" clearly understood by decision makers down through the organization? If not, the questions—and confusion—may be endless. ("Why are we installing this customer relationship management system?" "Why are we reorganizing?" "Why are we pulling out of Latin America?" "Are we streamlining our order-fulfillment process to establish a competitive advantage, to eliminate a competitive disadvantage, and/or to reduce costs?")

Chapter 2 discusses the identification of strategic initiatives.

2. FAILING TO TACKLE A MANAGEABLE NUMBER OF INITIATIVES

The most frequent trap into which organizations fall is initiative overload. A business, regardless of its nature, size, complexity, and infrastructure, has a finite project capacity. Money is limited, person-hours are limited, mind share is limited, and the change-absorption bandwidth is limited. Unaware of their organization's limitations, executives frequently launch more initiatives than can be effectively and efficiently implemented. The typical outcome? Twelve initiatives are adequately implemented and three end up as roadkill. A better result? The five most pivotal initiatives are spectacularly implemented.

Chapter 3 outlines a process for ensuring that you are tackling a manageable number of initiatives and that the ones you are pursuing have the highest strategic priority.

3. FAILING TO PUT THE RIGHT STRUCTURE IN PLACE

Most executives reorganize more than is necessary. You'll be happy to know that we are not necessarily proposing that you change your entire organization structure. However, you do want to ensure that your structure supports—or at least does not impede—the deployment of strategic initiatives.

Chapter 4 describes alternative structures that support the success of initiatives.

4. FAILING TO INSTALL A SUPPORTIVE "INITIATIVE ENVIRONMENT"

A high-priority initiative can be pulled (or dragged) through the organization in a way that leaves its contributors, other projects, and ongoing operations in need of life support. Attributes of a healthy culture include expectations, feedback, and reward systems that buttress initiative accomplishment without bludgeoning other activities.

Executives who tend to approach issues solely with a "systems and procedures" orientation unwittingly create a common cultural deficiency. As we argue in subsequent chapters, infrastructure, tools, and protocols are important to the success of initiatives; however, they are not enough. Initiative contributors at all levels are people who require the same care and feeding in the project environment as they need in their "day job." Initiatives involve change. Most people resist change or, at the very least, find it disorienting and anxiety producing. As a result, the implementation of initiatives requires that management pay more attention than usual to human factors.

Chapter 5 presents an approach for changing or buttressing those aspects of your culture that influence initiative success.

5. FAILING TO INVOLVE THE RIGHT PEOPLE IN THE RIGHT WAYS

Initiatives are only as effective as the people who populate them. Special projects should not be a refuge for people who are merely available or for those whose absence from ongoing operations is a blessing in disguise. A poorly positioned or unqualified sponsor, project manager, or set of team members can scuttle even the best-intentioned and best-designed project.

Chapter 6 describes the roles that should be played by the people whose skills, experience, information, brainpower, and commitment are necessary for initiative success. As a leader, you are one of those people.

6. FAILING TO USE A COMMON LANGUAGE FOR INITIATIVE MANAGEMENT

Most high-impact initiatives involve three or more people. The biggest involve dozens or even hundreds. If these people are to contribute effectively, they need to be able to communicate. To communicate effectively and efficiently, people from different departments and at different levels need the *lingua franca* of a shared process and lexicon.

Chapter 7 describes the basic features and benefits of a common initiative/project management process. More detail is provided in Appendix A.

7. FAILING TO INSTALL AN EFFECTIVE, EFFICIENT REPORTING AND MONITORING SYSTEM

A key executive responsibility is monitoring the performance of strategic initiatives and making midcourse corrections as needed. To carry out this responsibility, you need a reporting/oversight system that gives you the information you need without creating a draining bureaucracy.

Chapter 8 presents examples of reporting processes and formats that have worked for organizations in a variety of industries.

8. FAILING TO BE PATIENT

A wag once defined executives as "people with attention spans of 60 seconds or less." Whether or not you are a poster child for Adult Attention Deficit Disorder, you need to recognize that strategy implementation requires patience. Even if your strategy doesn't involve a major departure from the past, initiatives involving product development, market entry and exit, acquisitions, process improvement, curing a dysfunctional culture, or changing organization structure cannot be implemented overnight.

Throughout the chapters that follow, we will discuss steps you can take to keep your long-term eye on the most important balls, as in Figure 1-2.

YOUR ROLE IN STRATEGY IMPLEMENTATION

Some of these eight booby traps can be cleared only through personal action by senior executives. Others can be dealt with by managers farther down the line. However, since strategy implementation is the responsibility of you and your fellow executives, you must see that obstacles are identified and removed.

At its simplest level, success is a function of two factors: the quality of the strategy that is guiding the organization and the effectiveness and efficiency of the implementation of that strategy. This book focuses on the second factor. Executives have learned that exhortation is not enough. Implementation

FIGURE 1-2   The Seven Critical Success Factors for Strategy Implementation

is a function of the design and execution of initiatives. If your destination is change, initiatives are the vehicles that will take you there.

Your organization may be in the public or the private sector, product or service focused, domestic or international, large or small. You may run an entire organization, a business unit or division, a function, or a region. All of these types of organizations and executive roles share a common critical need: leadership. A key component of leadership is the generation and institutionalization of change. There are no changes more important than those that transform your strategic vision into action and, ultimately, into results. While the details of change implementation can be delegated, the guidance and responsibility cannot be. As you guide your organization through all the change and churn, remember that strategic initiatives drive that effort and will ultimately determine whether you master change or become its unwitting victim.

As an executive, you will rarely be a member of an initiative team. Only occasionally—for very high-priority or extremely sensitive initiatives—will you play the role of initiative/project manager. However, you should frequently play the role of initiative sponsor.

In our experience, the hallmark of strategy implementation is leadership. Figure 1-2 depicts seven factors that we have found to be essential for successful strategy implementation. As a leader, you need to play a variety of roles to ensure that these factors are present in your organization. The remainder of this book describes each of these roles: direction setter, decision maker, guide, communicator, energizer, barrier remover, and conflict resolver.

NOTES

1. In the vignette that opens each chapter, the executive and company names have been changed to maintain confidentiality.
2. Ken Belson, "Idei Failed to Get Sony to Focus on His Vision," *International Herald Tribune*, Mar. 9, 2005.
3. Wayne Bragg, "Why Carly?" *Connecticut Post*, Mar. 1, 2005.
4. Michael Beer and Russell Eisenstat, "How to Have an Honest Conversation About Your Business Strategy," *Harvard Business Review*, February 2004.
5. "Europe: Reinventing Lisbon," *Economist*, Feb. 1, 2005.
6. Ram Charan and Geoffrey Colvin, "Why CEOs Fail," *Fortune*, June 21, 1999.
7. For an exploration of strategic decision making, see Mike Freedman, *The Art and Discipline of Strategic Leadership* (New York: McGraw-Hill, 2003).

8. Alan Brache, *How Organizations Work: Taking a Holistic Approach to Organization Health* (New York: John Wiley & Sons, 2002).
9. Kevin Kelly, "New Rules for the New Economy," *Wired*, September 1997, p. 140.
10. The Standish Group, *Chaos Study*, 2004.
11. The Standish Group, *Chaos Study*, 1995.

C H A P T E R

2

SURVEYING THE INITIATIVE LANDSCAPE

*I*N MANY WAYS, ALFONSO RODRIQUEZ, *vice president of market-ing for Williams & Starkey's Grooming Products Division (GPD), is a typical executive; he is bright, has infectious energy, holds his people to lofty standards, and is famously impatient. His numbers look good, and he is proud of his department's talent, cus-tomer focus, and work ethic. Because he is a big thinker and a master communicator, many have him pegged as a future CEO.*

While GPD—largely as a result of its exemplary merchandis-ing and brand management—has become an industry benchmark, Alfonso is not satisfied. He believes that the organization should set its sights beyond incremental improvement and outperforming the competition on the current field of battle. He thinks that GPD can enjoy sustained double-digit growth if it can capitalize on a unique and time-limited opportunity to reinvent itself in a way that transforms the fickle and faddish personal products industry. Largely in response to Alfonso's hectoring, the GPD top team has formulated a strategy in which products are far more customized to the needs and preferences of local domestic and international markets, customers are more intimately involved in new product

19

development, guarantees of customer satisfaction go beyond any-
thing ever attempted in the personal products space, and all non-
core functions are outsourced, enabling GPD to focus on what it
does best.

Like many visionaries, Alfonso is less effective at execution.
He naively assumed that once the new, compelling strategy had
been communicated, people and systems would spontaneously
align themselves with it. But the nature and pace of implementa-
tion has failed to meet his expectations. While he is not sure why
these efforts have fallen short, he suspects that there are two pri-
mary causes. First, he thinks that both middle and senior man-
agers are so involved in day-to-day issues that they fail to make
the step-change improvements in both customer-interface and
back-office operations that the strategy demands. Second, he
thinks that the organization is disturbingly resistant to change.
The reaction to radical proposals tends to be "Here's why that
won't work" or "Good idea, but the timing isn't right" as opposed
to "How can we make that happen?" or, at least, "Let's take a
serious look at that." The culture embraces continuous improve-
ment, which is healthy, but shuns major initiatives, which is not.

Alfonso's colleagues have helped him understand that change
of this magnitude doesn't happen overnight. However, he still
believes that if the strategy is not implemented soon, the window
of opportunity will close. While he has learned that he shouldn't
expect to have scored yet, he sees no evidence that the ball is being
moved forward.

Maybe your situation is different from Alfonso's. You may
be experiencing initiative proliferation, not initiative paucity.
However, you and he have the same need: to make sure that
your register of potential initiatives includes everything that
needs to be done to implement your strategy.

Without a full slate of nominees, you can't be sure that you
will elect the critical few initiatives that will move your vision
from the meeting room to the marketplace. In Chapter 3, we
will present a process for setting priorities on and sequencing
projects. But first, we need a list of projects from which to

FIGURE 2-1   Initiative Identification: A Critical Success Factor
for Strategy Implementation

choose. This chapter focuses on the Initiative Identification
success factor, highlighted in Figure 2-1.

THE EXECUTIVE ROLE IN
STRATEGIC INITIATIVE IDENTIFICATION

As an executive, one of your central roles is identifying and
defining strategy implementation initiatives. You shouldn't
expect them to "bubble up"; you and your leadership-team
colleagues are the only people who understand the strategy

profoundly enough, who have the panoramic context, and who have the power and influence to get people working on the right things.

A global household appliance manufacturer was not realizing the financial and nonfinancial benefits that it had expected from its recent acquisition of four competitors. The newly expanded company was experiencing increases in operating costs, late deliveries, repeat service calls, bad debt, and staff turnover. The CEO was getting no comforting answer to his question: "What is—or is not—going on?" He asked us to help him and his team identify and define a set of on-target initiatives.

As a backdrop for our work, we asked a basic question: "What are the root causes of these five problems?" The executives thought they knew the causes; unfortunately, the cause that each of them "knew" for a given deficiency was different from that "known" by the others. For example, one executive was convinced that the cost issue was a result of ill-defined business processes. Another offered to bet her paycheck on a talent deficit as the cause. A third was sure that the culprit was excessive overhead.

To commission the right initiatives, we had to get at the truth. Our analysis showed that

- In their zeal to address every market need within their capabilities and to motivate the product champions in the acquired companies, the executives had not "sunset" any products. They had also significantly increased the funding for product development. The primary reason that the company hadn't met its cost-reduction goals was that its product portfolio was too complex and was riddled with substandard performers. Our analysis revealed that 56 percent of the company's products were producing only 5 percent of sales and, after costs were appropriately allocated, were losing money.

- The delivery failures and bad debt were due to poor integration of the business processes of the five companies. Redrawing the organization chart had taken precedence over redesigning critical business processes such as order fulfillment, distribution, and billing.

- Combining the five customer-service functions had not addressed the process used to handle incoming calls. The field-service engineers had the skills to make the repairs. However, because the help desk personnel failed to ask the right questions during the initial call, the engineers often arrived at the customer site without the right parts or did not have sufficient time to complete the repair. They needed a second visit to finish their work.

- Executives had anticipated a modest level of employee turnover after the acquisitions. However, contrary to their expectations, they lost an alarming number of experienced, productive people. These losses had little to do with people's aversion to change or the job market's demand for their skills. It was more the result of rumors of site closings and people's natural desire to jump before being pushed.

This analysis uncovered needs that resulted in the identification of 31 potential initiatives. To ensure focus and coordination, these initiatives were grouped into eight buckets (which the executive team called "programs"): marketing (which included a project to reduce product complexity), logistics (which included a project to redesign the order-fulfillment process), finance (which included a project to improve the billing and collections process), business administration (which included a call center skill-development project), human resources (which included an acquisition-integration communication project), sales management, service, and information technology.

Most of these 31 projects were new, and quite a few of them would never have been identified if the top team had not gone through a systematic process of identifying and defining initiatives. Other projects were already underway, but they were insufficiently linked, sequenced, sponsored, and staffed.

Through this effort, the executive team learned that the sequence of steps in strategic Initiative Identification should be

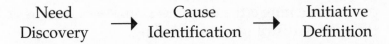

Need   Cause   Initiative
Discovery   →   Identification   →   Definition

These executives were wise enough to avoid jumping into all 31 initiatives, which they knew would bring the company to its knees. To whittle the list down to those that could be successfully accomplished within a three-year strategic time frame, they followed the process outlined in Chapter 3. Without disciplined Initiative Identification, they would not have isolated the proper field of projects to be considered, nor would they have had a solid basis for knowing which projects addressed which needs, and which ones needed to be carried out before others.

STRATEGIC INITIATIVE CHECKLIST

We have found the following checklist, which covers the waterfront of strategy implementation, to be useful in Initiative Identification. Every item that you check, indicating a yes answer to the question, highlights an area that requires action. Your top team should decide whether that need (1) is being adequately met by an existing initiative, (2) demands the revision of an existing initiative, or (3) suggests a potential new initiative. We say "potential" because you probably do not have the resources to launch them all, at least not in the next 12 months. So, all candidates will be fed into the hopper for evaluation during Initiative Priority Setting.

❑   Do you need to research or monitor the external environment (e.g., competition, regulatory policy, the economy) more formally in light of the assumptions that underpin your strategy?

❑   Does your strategy require the introduction or sunset of any products?

❑   Does your strategy require market entry or exit?

❑   Does your strategy include any "let's explore" areas that require market research?

❑   Does your strategy require a new thrust for your marketing?

❑   Do the competitive advantages that will fuel your future success require the design or redesign of any business processes? If so, which ones? (For example, you need to enhance your competitive advantage by streamlining your distribution process, or you need to overcome a competitive disadvantage by installing a customer support process.)

❑   Do the competitive advantages that will fuel your future success require the creation or enhancement of any skills? If so, which ones? (For example, you need to improve your salespeople's ability to identify customer needs.)

❑   Does your strategy require relocation or the opening or closing of any plants, offices, or labs?

❑   Does your strategy require the investigation of any potential acquisitions or alliances?

❑   Does your strategy highlight a need to investigate a new technology?

❑   Does your strategy require (re)branding?

❑   Does your strategy require the investigation of possible intellectual-property protection?

❑   Does your strategy indicate that you should be outsourcing functions that are currently performed internally or insourcing functions that are currently performed externally?

❑   To ensure that you are tracking the viability and implementation of your strategy, do you need to measure performance that is not currently being measured? (For example, you need to supplement your measurement of financial results with measures that capture new-product performance and customer satisfaction.)

❑   Does your strategy require you to better manage knowledge through the use of databases that are integrated, up

to date, and easily accessed? (For example, you need customer information that is more comprehensive, more
current, and sorted differently.)

❑ Does your strategy require you to better manage knowledge through forums for person-to-person information
sharing? (For example, you need to institute a mecha-
nism for getting salespeople together, face to face or at
least voice to voice, to share their experiences in selling
follow-on services.)

❑ Does your strategy require an examination of alternative
organizational structures? (For example, since you are
going to grow by penetrating offshore markets, you need
to determine whether there is a structure that better supports international expansion.)

❑ Does your strategy require improvement in—or at least
an analysis of the health of—your culture? (For example,
since you will be developing and commercializing new
products, you want to make sure that your culture supports innovation.)

❑ Do you need to align your operational planning and
budgeting with your strategy?

❑ Does your strategy require changes to the depth,
breadth, roles, or skills of the organization's leadership?
(For example, you need to strengthen the top team members' ability to interact with the media, legislatures, the
public, and nongovernmental organizations.)

❑ Do you need substrategies at the business unit, product
line, or functional levels?

❑ Do you need a well-orchestrated game plan for communicating the strategy to internal and external audiences?

All these questions assume that you have a strategy that
answers the questions listed in Chapter 1. If you don't, your
first initiative should be to formulate or update your strategy.
Then, you can focus on implementation.

As you can see from these questions, we are coming at Initiative Identification from a strategic perspective rather than an issue perspective. You may have a revenue issue, a profitability issue, a customer-image issue, a market-share issue, a productivity issue, a technology-obsolescence issue, or an employee-retention issue. However, before you launch a well-intentioned but overly global and fuzzy initiative in any of these areas, you should identify the underlying cause(s) of the problem or opportunity, and then determine whether the issue is strategic or tactical.

A revenue shortfall that is rooted in your organization's inability to bring successful new products to market is a different challenge from a shortfall that is caused by a talent deficit in your business developers. A profitability issue that is a function of your pricing must be tackled differently from one that is caused by spiraling costs.

We are not saying that tactical issues are second-class citizens. Some tactical issues are high-impact, urgent, and complex enough to merit executive involvement. Some of your tactical issues—for example, a need to mollify a dissatisfied customer, update your price list, or submit a bid on a major new piece of business—may be higher priority, or at least more urgent, than some of your strategic issues. However, they are a breed apart.

Unfortunately, tactical issues frequently take precedence over strategic issues. The president of a retail chain for whom we have facilitated strategy formulation and implementation sessions summed up the concern of many executives when he said, "My biggest challenge is finding a way to avoid being consumed with the 'day-to-day.' My executive team and I tend to get tied up in the issues that are making the most noise. We need to get better at managing the trade-off between what is urgent and what is critical."

Our focus throughout this book is on issues that have risen above the "day-to-day" to become the ones that are most critical to your organization's future: those that must be resolved in order to implement your strategy.

DEFINITION OF STRATEGIC INITIATIVES

You have descended from the mountaintop with the strategic tablets, and you are fired up to make it happen. You assess the key components of your strategy and the potential initiative each suggests. For example:

- *Market.* You identified high-income urban couples between the ages of 30 and 45 as the market that represents the greatest potential for your products. You define an initiative that includes (1) evaluating the benefits and features of your products to make sure that they address the needs of that market, (2) assessing your marketing to make sure that it "speaks" to that target demographic, (3) establishing and tracking performance against companywide goals for your sales to and share of that market, and (4) reflecting those goals in the measurement of the processes, departments, and individuals that contribute to revenue generation from that market.

- *Technology.* You identified the accuracy, speed, and "human touch" dimensions of technical support as a future competitive advantage. You define an initiative in which processes and skills are upgraded so that you move from competitive parity to competitive advantage in this area.

- *Acquisition.* You decided to get into an adjacent market and concluded that the most effective and efficient way to do so is through an acquisition of a niche company. You define an initiative that includes identifying and evaluating potential acquirees, making contact, negotiating the terms, performing the due diligence, consummating the deal, and integrating the acquired company.

- *Outsourcing.* Most of your manufacturing is done externally, and you have decided to outsource the remainder. While you will use the supplier that handles the bulk of your production today, this decision has raised key questions, including "Do you have a structure that enables you to interface smoothly with your manufacturing partner?" and "How can you ensure appropriate oversight without excessive headcount?" You define an initiative to evaluate alternative structures for managing your relationship with your manufacturing partner.

- *Culture.* As a bridge from your strategy to its implementation, you and your colleagues have defined what your culture should be. The hallmarks of that culture are innovation, flexibility, and controlled risk-taking. You define an initiative that includes analyzing your current culture and closing any gaps.

- *Communication.* You recognize that strategies don't spontaneously combust. Nor can they be implemented solely through the hard work of the leadership team. You recognize that a key element in implementing the strategy is communication. If key external stakeholders and people at all levels internally don't understand the vision—the what, the why, and the what it means to me—they will be unable to play the appropriate role in its implementation. You define an initiative that encompasses the process, roles, and timing of strategy communication.

These are just examples. An initial list of potential strategic initiatives often contains 30 or 40 candidates. The description of each should include its scope (what's in and what's out), its outputs (what it will produce), and its benefits (what it will accomplish). Stated specifically and concisely in this way, each initiative will be able to vie with the others for the company's precious time and money.

DEVELOPING THE STRATEGIC MASTER PROJECT PLAN

Strategy implementation ultimately coalesces in what we call a *Strategic Master Project Plan*, which is a compilation of all the initiatives that need to be deployed to achieve the vision. This "plan of plans" is the top team's view of all the pieces of the strategy implementation puzzle. If used wisely, it avoids both fragmentation of the strategy implementation effort and issue clog. Its initiatives may be in any of the areas suggested by the questions in the checklist that appears earlier in this chapter.

The initiatives in your Strategic Master Project Plan may come from any of the areas suggested by the questions in the checklist. The final plan is the product of both the Initiative Identification that has been discussed in this chapter and the Initiative Priority Setting that will be covered in Chapter 3.

STRATEGY IMPLEMENTATION INITIATIVES: A CASE STUDY

An international deluxe hotel group asked us to identify and clarify the portfolio of strategic initiatives that would deliver the step change needed to overcome lackluster business performance.

The top team had recently completed its strategy formulation. During that project, team members had identified and set priorities on the services the hotel group would offer, defined the markets on which it would focus, and described the competitive advantages that would enable it to win in its chosen space. The team was brought down from the giddy heights of visioning when it had to confront the need to identify the full range of initiatives necessary to achieve its new strategic thrust and goals.

Using the framework of the Enterprise Model, introduced in Chapter 1 and repeated here as Figure 2-2, a number of the change requirements jumped off the pages of the strategy. They included the following:

- For too long, the *leadership* of the business had been focused on defending the company against a protracted takeover bid. Thankfully, that attempt had failed and was now history. The new strategy would be successfully implemented only through the "power and the passion" of the top team. New leaders needed to be found, and existing leaders needed to be redirected and energized.

- A related issue concerned the role of a formerly hostile *shareholder*. Although the cessation of takeover activities was the catalyst for developing the new strategy, *organi-*

FIGURE 2-2   The Enterprise Model Variables in Which a Hotel Chain Identified Strategy Implementation Initiatives

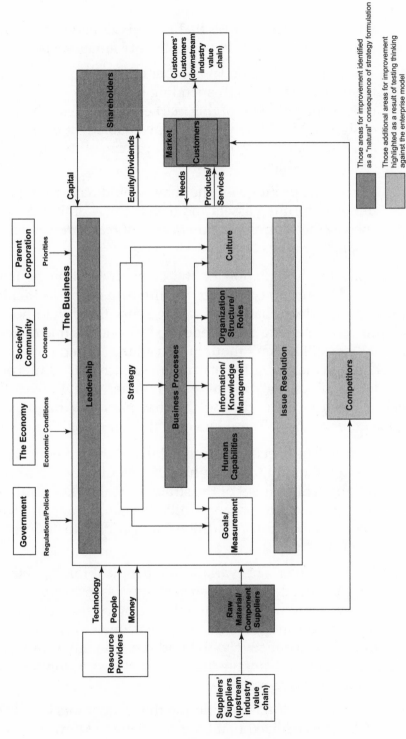

31

zation structures and roles had to be redefined to formalize
the new relationship between the old antagonists.

- The strategy identified a number of new ways to reach a
  target market: the high-spending business traveler. To
  unlock the potential of this market, the top team had to
  design and build new technology-enabled *business
  processes* for the distribution and pricing of the accommo-
  dation "product."

- To meet its profit goals, the chain would have to shed
  underperforming assets and develop economies of scale,
  such as the centralized purchasing of *raw materials and
  supplies* for all its hotels.

While the articulation of the company's strategy made
these and many other change requirements easy to identify,
the executive team had the nagging sense that it had not yet
identified everything that needed to be done. As one member
put it, "We still haven't thought into all the corners."

Through the discipline of examining each of the Enterprise
Model variables, they identified a number of initiatives that
hadn't been obvious during the first pass and might have
gone unrecognized. These included the following:

- *Culture.* The executives realized that they had not given
  enough thought to the culture that would have to underpin the achievement of the strategic goals. They realized
  that only a culture-change initiative could transform customer service from "traditional and stuffy" to "informal
  and friendly."

- *Issue resolution.* This variable got people thinking about
  the consistency with which customer issues were
  resolved and the degree to which employees were given
  the latitude and skills to resolve customer problems
  quickly and effectively. To build the company's desired
  competitive advantage in this area, the team commissioned an issue-resolution initiative.

- *Competitors.* While considering the competitors box, the
  executives realized that their competitive knowledge was

made up entirely of assumptions and anecdotal experiences, not facts. They decided to build systems for competitive intelligence gathering/analysis and benchmarking.

The Enterprise Model provided these executives with a framework that helped them identify everything they needed to do in order to move the organization from where it was strategically to where it needed to be. The resulting change portfolio contained 52 initiatives, which were grouped into eight programs.

As in the case of the appliance manufacturer cited earlier in this chapter, you may be alarmed by the number of programs and projects that were identified by the top team. However, these initiatives were phased in anywhere from several months to as much as one year after the first wave. In addition, many projects that were underway before the strategy formulation were subsumed, delayed, or terminated. Through the priority-setting and sequencing process presented in Chapter 3, the top team ensured that the organization didn't bite off more than it could chew.

THE INITIATIVE IDENTIFICATION PROCESS

While anyone should be able to propose a strategic initiative, an organization needs a protocol for submitting and evaluating potential projects. Most executives with whom we work find that a one-page "Project Initiation Proposal" imposes the discipline that is needed. That form typically includes the information indicated by the categories in Figure 2-3.

BEWARE OF BUDGETING SEASON

While an initiative can be born at any time, there is typically a surge of new-project proposals during and immediately following budget development. At that time, a disproportionate number of projects are conceived, pitched, and either approved or rejected. During that peak season, you should take particular care to ensure that the strategic initiatives are not underre-

FIGURE 2-3   A Sample Project Initiation Proposal

Project Name	
Initiator	
Proposed Sponsor	
Proposed Project Manager	
Issue(s)/Need(s) to Be Addressed	
Benefits to Be Realized	
Estimated Costs	
Estimated Personnel Time	
Performance against Priority-Setting Criteria	
Approvals Required	

sourced or lost in a sea of tactical pursuits. In a budget battle between strategic and operational initiatives, the latter often prevail, particularly given the immediate pressures facing managers at all levels. During these deliberations, you and your executive colleagues have to be strong stewards of the strategy.

WHERE DO YOU START?

Here is an understandable reaction to the strategy implementation needs we have explored:

"I know my organization. I am not a Pollyanna. Our strategy requires improvement in all the areas depicted in the Enterprise Model. I've got leadership needs and business process needs and culture needs and right on down the list. If I were to launch initiatives in each of these areas, I would drown. Where do I start?"

Initiative overload—the "eyes bigger than the stomach" syndrome—is a common ailment, particularly among executives who lack an understanding of what it takes to accomplish projects. Almost as ubiquitous is a gnawing concern that the projects that are underway are not those with the highest payback. As an executive, you are responsible for assessing the merit of all types of initiatives that address strategic issues. In some cases, you conceive a project; in other situations, someone recommends one to you. To play both the initiator role and the evaluator role, you need a disciplined process to determine whether an initiative is worth pursuing and, if so, where it falls in the priorities and how it can be funded and staffed. We devote the next chapter to this critical, executive-level process.

3

PREVENTING
INITIATIVE OVERLOAD

KATHERINE DEVOY, EXECUTIVE VICE PRESIDENT OF FINANCE
AND ADMINISTRATION *of the online travel agency Custom-
travel.com, thinks in metaphors. While she is stimulated by
Customtravel's goals and energy, she envisions the company as the
old woman in the shoe, who "had so many children she didn't know
what to do." The old woman spends most of her time in the maternity
ward, either in labor or having just given birth. In this case, the
progeny are projects.*

*A newcomer to Customtravel, Katherine is an information tech-
nology–industry veteran who has never seen so many special initiatives. To extend her breeding metaphor, it's as if someone has been
spiking the water coolers with fertility drugs. Projects are being created by the old and the young, the wise and the clueless, first-time
parents and those who are already raising more "children" than they
can afford. While some are being nurtured in a caring, supportive
environment, most are not.*

*Katherine doesn't think that any organization the size of Cus-
tomtravel—at any level of maturity—can successfully implement so
many projects. Customtravel is littered with project roadkill. Some*

fell behind the filing cabinets and have never been seen again. Some are in dysfunctional conflict with others. Many are consuming alarming quantities of time and money. Some come to fruition too late to meet the intended need. Some crumble under the weight of unrealistic expectations. Many are noble but never realize their potential.

She is sure that the company has enough talent to successfully deploy a small number of highly successful initiatives. However, the diffusion of money, time, and brainpower is preventing most projects from achieving their objectives.

As a finance person, Katherine is understandably troubled by this dilution and misapplication of resources. As a member of the executive team, however, she has a bigger concern. Customtravel has to remain strategically nimble in an environment of rapid change and cutthroat competition. She fears that the company's strategy— which is centered on responsiveness to customers and low fares for novel vacation packages—is at risk of remaining a compelling, but unrealized, dream. She is convinced that strategic initiatives are not getting the visibility, the funding, and the staffing that they require.

Initiatives are the vehicles for implementing strategy. If you have completed the Initiative Identification process described in Chapter 2, you probably have the haunting feeling that implementing all the projects that you identified would require an organization the size of the Chinese Army and funding that exceeds the gross domestic product of Scandinavia.

It would be easy—if not painless—to slash and burn; after all, making tough choices is a challenge you face daily as a leader. Before you do so, however, we suggest that you ask yourself two pivotal questions:

- How many projects should you eliminate? Or, more positively, how many can you take on?

- How can you ensure that the projects that survive will be the ones that deserve to make the cut?

You have a personal investment portfolio that contains your stocks, bonds, tangibles, real estate, and other financial

FIGURE 3-1   Initiative Priority Setting: A Critical Success Factor for Strategy Implementation

assets. Your company or agency has a portfolio of products and services that it offers. Similarly, your organization should have a *project* portfolio that contains every initiative that is planned or underway. Just like managing your investment portfolio, managing your project portfolio requires solid answers to two questions: "How much is in there?" and "How much of it belongs there?" This chapter outlines a process called Optimal Project Portfolio (OPP) that will enable you to answer these questions with confidence. While we will continue to focus on the initiatives that play a role in implementing strategy, the OPP process forces you to examine such initiatives within the context of your organization's entire project landscape.

HOW HEALTHY IS YOUR PROJECT PORTFOLIO?

First of all, do you know the current state of your portfolio? Specifically

> Do you—or does anyone else in your organization—know how many projects are afoot and how much money they are consuming?

Even if your organization's projects are not neatly documented in one place, you may think that you are close enough to operations to have a reasonably accurate idea of how many projects are underway at any given time. You might be surprised.

Remember the vice president of product development we spoke about in Chapter 1? He thought that there were 25 to 30 projects in the pipeline when, in fact, there were more than 200 in progress. In another case, the vice president of marketing of a European beverage company estimated that his organization had 35 marketing initiatives at various stages, from just initiated to nearly completed. After we investigated the situation, we astonished him with the news that there were no fewer than 130 projects underway. About 100 of these projects were not significant resource drains. However, some had been launched and remained in limbo. Most were consuming at least the time it took to enter "no progress" on the monthly project status report. Most disturbingly, some of these invisible initiatives actually had greater potential than higher-visibility/higher-investment projects. Furthermore, the marketing vice president had no idea how many initiatives the organization could manage. It was analogous to his wanting to rationalize his personal financial portfolio without knowing how much money he had to invest.

> Do you know your project capacity? In other words, do you know how many person-years of project work you—and those for whom you are responsible—can take on without compromising the performance of other projects and ongoing operations)?

Most investors favor an asset allocation approach that puts the proper emphasis on each sector and style of investment, given their particular strategy: growth, income, or capital preservation. Similarly, it is imperative that you consider how well you have allocated your project assets. In that light

> Do you have the right mix of strategic and tactical initiatives? Growth-driven and cost-driven initiatives? Product-oriented and market-oriented initiatives? Customer-touch and back-office initiatives? Long-term and quick-hit initiatives?

The balance of strategic and tactical initiatives is particularly important. Executives should ensure that all "operational excellence" projects support the strategy and that the portfolio includes other projects that are solely focused on implementing the strategy.

ESTABLISHING AN OPTIMAL PROJECT PORTFOLIO

If your answers to these three questions cause chronic pain, you will be pleased to know that there is a cure. Initiative creation and deployment can be disciplined, controlled, rewarded, and respected. And it's worth the effort: Exemplary portfolio management can make as significant a contribution to your competitive advantage as world-class manufacturing, customer service, financial management, and human resource management.

For much of the Initiative Management process, executives should be sponsors and monitors, leaving the nitty-gritty to those at lower levels. However, to ensure that your projects are strategically focused, the front end of that process—establishing an Optimal Project Portfolio—requires your hands-on involvement.

A PLATFORM FOR OPTIMAL PROJECT PORTFOLIO CREATION

Before you can establish your Optimal Project Portfolio, you need to understand your project portfolio's current state, warts and all. The questions you will want to answer include the following:

- Who initiates projects? What normally triggers projects?

- Who approves projects? What are the approval criteria? What is the approval process?

- Who determines a project's funding requirements? Who determines the staffing requirements? How do resources get allocated to a project?

- Do initiatives have senior-level sponsors? If so, how are these sponsors identified? What role(s) are they expected to play?

- How are project managers selected? What role(s) are they expected to play? How are they trained?

- How are the members of initiative teams selected? What role(s) are they expected to play? How are they trained?

- How are target populations (the set of people influenced by the outcomes of initiatives) identified? What involvement do they have at the beginning and in the course of projects?

- What process, methods, and tools are used for defining projects, planning projects, monitoring projects, and closing out projects?

- How is project success measured?

- What is the general perception of projects at all levels?

- How readily does the organization embrace the changes required by major projects? What factors tend to encourage receptivity to change? What factors cause resistance to change?

- What is your initiative track record? Do initiatives typically achieve their objectives? Stay within their budgets? Meet their target completion dates?

The accurate—if not entirely satisfying—answer to all of these questions may be, "It depends." If this is the case, your responses should reflect the most frequent or representative situations. The purpose of this assessment is not to flagellate yourself; it is to establish the baseline environment in which your project portfolio will be launched. It goes beyond folklore and war stories to provide an evidence-based understanding of both what is working and what needs to be changed. It pinpoints ground zero: the "you are here" from which the strategy implementation journey must begin.

Katherine from Customtravel.com, the company whose project quagmire opens this chapter, was able to get "overall project status" on the agenda of an executive committee meeting. Answering the questions just listed was a sobering experience. The committee's assessment revealed that projects were out of control. Almost anyone could launch a project without justification or approval, an estimate of resource consumption, an evaluation of capacity, or reconciliation with other projects. Roles were unfilled or unclear. Monitoring was sporadic. Because of the diffusion of time, money, and mind share, projects generally fell short of expectations, failed to meet deadlines, and overran their budgets. It became obvious that progress toward implementing Customtravel's strategy had been minimal.

Unpleasant as the findings were, Katherine had achieved her objective: getting her colleagues to recognize that project proliferation and underperformance were serious, executive-level issues and that it was essential that top management establish an Optimal Project Portfolio.

THE OPTIMAL PROJECT PORTFOLIO (OPP) PROCESS

In keeping with our strategy implementation focus, we could suggest that you limit your prioritization to those initiatives that are required to execute your strategy. Big mistake!

Strategic initiatives must be prioritized within the context of the full portfolio because some tactical initiatives may be higher priority than strategic initiatives and because all projects draw from the same human and financial resource pool.

OPP STEP 1: DEVELOP PROJECT PRIORITIZATION CRITERIA

You now want to focus on the future. The first step is to erect a platform for rationalizing and fortifying your project portfolio. The planks in that platform are the criteria that you will use to select and set priorities for current and potential projects. At their broadest level, such criteria typically fall into these categories:

- Implement the strategy (the umbrella over a number of the other criteria)

- Increase sales

- Establish/widen a competitive advantage or eliminate a competitive disadvantage

- Increase customer satisfaction

- Reduce cost

- Increase employee satisfaction/retention

- Ensure regulatory compliance

- Protect safety

To customize the criteria to your situation:

- Delete the categories that don't apply. For example, regulatory compliance may not be a project-priority discriminator for you at this time.

- Add criteria that are unique to your situation. For example, you may want to include one that gives extra credit to projects that involve quick wins or have high—or low—external visibility.

- Assign weights that will enable some criteria to exert greater influence on your decision.

To ensure that your project portfolio covers an appropriate waterfront, you will want to strike the right, though not necessarily equal, balance between criteria that are strategic and tactical, short term and long term, externally focused and internally focused, and structure/system/policy focused and people focused.

To ensure that all who will be affected by the prioritization understand your criteria, we suggest including an "as evidenced by" definition for each criterion. For example, "Maximize customer satisfaction, as evidenced by attrition percentage, number of complaints, and survey ratings."

These criteria should not be established in a vacuum or as an academic exercise. Keep in mind their purpose: Your top team will use them in Step 4 of the OPP process as the basis for determining the priority of current and potential initiatives. To forge maximum consensus, we recommend that the group hammer them out. As you develop criteria, continually keep in mind the phrase, "We want to invest more time and money in those projects that _____."

For example, the top team of a multinational appliance manufacturer/marketer used these criteria as the basis for the prioritization of its Western European division initiatives:

- Deliver increased market share

- Improve profitability

- Reduce operating costs

- Help us become the supplier of choice for retailers

- Empower team members

- Deliver consumer delight

- Streamline business processes

A pharmaceutical company determined its project priorities using these criteria:

- Maximize customer benefits

- Minimize legal/regulatory exposure

- Minimize product cost
- Optimize cost-benefit
- Maximize continuity of supply
- Optimize manufacturing capacity

Customtravel's executive committee established these criteria:

We will give the highest priority to those current and proposed projects that

- *Implement one or more components of the corporate strategy.*
- *Maximize contribution to revenue generation.*
- *Maximize contribution to profitability.*
- *Extend our competitive advantage in transaction speed.*
- *Enhance the Customtravel brand.*
- *Have a positive impact on employee satisfaction.*
- *Are likely to generate both quick wins and long-term benefits.*
- *Maximize the odds of success.*

OPP STEP 2: ANALYZE RESOURCE CAPACITY

It is not unusual for an organization to launch 40,000 hours of strategic initiatives in a year in which it has only 15,000 hours to devote to all its projects—both strategic and tactical. That gap cannot be closed by working harder or smarter. Barring a loaves-and-fishes-like divine intervention, something must give. Either the initiatives or ongoing operations are going to suffer.

Some organizations, such as NASA, Dreamworks, McKinsey, most advertising agencies, and most law firms, are totally project-driven; their project capacity is the same as their overall resource capacity. But in most organizations, projects exist over and above daily operations, which makes your project bandwidth less obvious.

You and your executive colleagues were front and center during Step 1 of OPP, establishing prioritization criteria. In Step 2, you engage one or more analysts. Through interviews, observation, job/goal review, work-product review, and application of experience and judgment, the analysts will derive a directionally correct estimate of project capacity. This estimate will include not only the number of people-hours by organization unit, but also the availability of machinery, facilities, and materials.

Simply stating that Initiative A will require X person-hours will not be sufficient to guide your assignment of staff. To be of maximum value, your capacity estimate will need to be categorized in a way that facilitates resource-allocation decisions. For example, you may want to specify each project's requirements by job type (engineers, financial analysts), by skill (hotel guest check-in, foreign currency exchange), by proficiency or experience (masters, apprentices), or even by personality type (innovators, implementers).

Beware! This step can become an analytical sinkhole. Note that we've described the estimate as needing to be only directionally correct. While people may need to complete time sheets for a couple of weeks to avoid out-of-the-blue guessing, the value of getting capacity to the third decimal place does not justify the investment.

For example, we were asked to bring clarity and focus to the project portfolio of the human resources (HR) and organization development department of a fast-moving consumer goods manufacturing and distribution company. The pain in this department was particularly acute. Project performance was poor, which came as no surprise to anyone on the staff. However, interviews with the department's internal customers brought to the surface the universal perception that this function consistently worked on the wrong things. This was news to the people involved.

Determining project bandwidth was a challenge in this organization because the time allocated to each employee's day job was not recorded or predictable. Not wanting to launch an exhaustive study that would inordinately delay decision making, we asked a sample of employees a simple set of questions about their current and historic project participation and the skills they contributed to those projects. The answers gave department management an accurate enough estimate of capacity to appropriately size the department's portfolio.

Before Customtravel could decide which projects should be jettisoned or deferred and which of the remainder should receive the greatest emphasis, its executives needed to know how much time could be devoted to projects without impeding day-to-day operations. They tapped two of the company's sharpest young staff people to calculate the number of hours required from each department to achieve the expected level of day-to-day performance—to keep the trains running. Subtracting that number from total available work hours yielded project capacity.

The top team experienced the same kinds of "ahas" that come to individuals who, as part of a loan application process, document their monthly expenses for the first time. Once they became aware that a remarkably low number of hours were available for project work, the team had a reasonable basis for initiative rationalization, staffing levels, and outsourcing decisions.

Now that you have defined the filter in the funnel, you are ready to determine the amount of project work that will fit through its mesh.

OPP STEP 3: GATHER AND ORGANIZE INFORMATION ON CURRENT PROJECTS

This step begins with the executives agreeing on the definition of *project*. We define a project as "a set of interdependent nonrepetitive activities directed toward a goal." However, that definition doesn't specify size. You don't want your portfolio analysis to be clogged with every five-person-day project. You want to focus on the initiatives that will have the greatest impact and will consume significant resources. For example, the human resources department cited in OPP Step 2 considered only projects that would have an elapsed time of more than six weeks and would consume more than 10 person-days and/or $10,000.

The remainder of OPP Step 3, like Step 2, is carried out by one or more analysts with a penchant for detail, forensic skills, project management experience, and a willingness to pry. The process they should follow is

- Identify the projects that are currently underway, those that have been proposed and approved but not yet launched, and those that have been recommended but not yet sanctioned. If, as is typical, these projects have not been consolidated on a single spreadsheet or whiteboard, the analysts may have to do a fair amount of digging.

- For each project, they should answer these questions:
  - What is the name (title) of this project?
  - What is the purpose of this project? In 25 words or less, how will this project contribute to our success?
  - What are the deliverables (outputs) of this project?
  - In what phase (definition, planning, or implementation) is this project?
  - Who is the sponsor? Who is the project manager? Who is on the project team? Who are the stakeholders? What roles are being played by each?
  - With as much precision as we can muster with a reasonable amount of time and effort, how many person-weeks/months/years is the project currently absorbing? How much money is it costing?
  - It is not unusual to identify a project for which some of this information does not exist or is not documented. Before proceeding, the analyst may need to capture it. This part of the process is quite simple if the organization uses a project initiation form such as the one described in Chapter 2.

- Develop a summary of the current project landscape that contains the information just listed, sorted by
  - *Project type.* For example, product development projects, marketing projects, and customer-service

projects. Or, revenue-growth projects, cost-reduction projects, and safety projects. Or, Product A projects, Product B projects, and Product C projects. Or, strategic projects and operational improvement projects.

- *Resource type.* What categories of people from each department or site are dedicated to project work? What machines? Which facilities? How much money?
- *Time.* When are the projects scheduled to begin and end, and when will the resources be needed?

If executives have put solid effort into OPP Step 1, their life will be considerably easier in Step 3. A good set of project portfolio criteria, even though it was developed with the future ("to be") in mind, can and should provide a focus and framework for capturing the as-is information. For example, an "enhance-the-brand" criterion can cause you to ask, "What brand-building projects are currently underway?" Your "reduce cost" criterion can trigger, "What cost-reduction initiatives are afoot?"

This step is frequently an eye-opener. For example, before the human resources team cited in Step 2 went through Step 3 of the process, the vice president had indicated that there were "no more than 20" current projects. She was alarmed when we unearthed 63.

After a few sotto voce comments about devoting resources to an unforecasted project to determine the level of project activity, the Customtravel top team assigned OPP Step 3 to the same analysts who had made the project capacity calculations in Step 2. The analysts captured project definitions—many of which hadn't existed, even for formal, high-visibility initiatives—and estimated the current and future resource consumption for each of the projects that was underway. They included initiatives that were planned but had not yet been launched and those that had been proposed but not yet approved.

As they wrapped their arms around the current level of project activity, the team had a predictable but valuable insight. As in most organizations, the project plate was overflowing. No matter how hearty the appetite, gratification had to be postponed on some and abandoned completely on others. Some food had to be thrown away or put in a doggie bag for another meal.

OPP STEP 4: EVALUATE THE PROJECT PORTFOLIO

You now have a clear idea of what is going into the project-portfolio funnel. You have the information that will enable you to thoroughly and fairly evaluate each project against the objectives you established in OPP Step 2. In Step 4, the executive team goes through the wrenching but necessary and enlightening exercise that produces these decisions:

- The projects that should be combined.

- The projects that are "go" and those that are "no-go."

- The projects that are "go," but that will be deferred until resources become available.

- The priority of the "go" projects.

- The sequence of the "go" projects. (Some projects may be able to run in parallel; some may need to follow others.)

This is also the step during which you and your executive team make necessary adjustments to the project definition, objectives, roles, and resource allocation.

A critical output of this step is the plan to communicate the project-portfolio decisions to all stakeholders. This communication must answer the questions "What?" "Why?" "How?" and "What does it mean to me?"

The appliance company cited in OPP Step 1 initially intended to embark on the full complement of 77 projects that were underway or approved. Members of the top team thought that they merely needed to set priorities and schedules. However, after going through Steps 3 through 5, they determined that they could tackle only 36 of those projects; the others were either eliminated or deferred until resources became available. Thirty-six initiatives may appear to be too many, and in some organizations it would be. But not for an organization as large as the appliance company. Its initiatives did not draw on the same resource pool. Many of the projects did not require executive team oversight. And, implementation was spread over the three years of the strategic time frame.

During this process, the learning is as valuable as the output. When the consumer goods human resources team went through OPP Step 4, the project that emerged as the second-highest priority was one that aligned the company's attendance-monitoring process with the European Union's Working Time Directive requirements. Before the top team's OPP deliberations, the vice president of human resources had been completely unaware that this project was underway in the bowels of her department!

During this step, the Customtravel executives earned their pay. They used the criteria from OPP Step 1 and their capacity constraints from Step 2 to make decisions on the current project portfolio as captured in Step 3. They eliminated, combined, subordinated, deferred, and set priorities. They reduced the corporatewide project list from 41 to 6. They ensured that the survivors had the sponsorship, project management, and resources to maximize the odds of success. They identified seven other projects as the next wave, to be launched or relaunched when additional time and money became available. To a person, they felt that they had never had a firmer grip on the special-initiative aspect of their business. More importantly, they were confident that Customtravel's strategic initiatives were being afforded the priority and resources they deserved.

OPP STEP 5: IMPLEMENT AN ONGOING PROJECT-PORTFOLIO-MANAGEMENT PROCESS

Project portfolio management pays significant dividends only if it becomes an ongoing process. The questions to be answered in Step 5 are

- Should an executive team be assigned responsibility for overseeing and guiding projects from initiation to closeout? The membership of this "project-portfolio-management committee" often comprises the same people as that of the organization's top team. Its formalization as a committee ensures that its members meet regularly with their project hats on.

- Should you create a "project office," which may be as modest as a fraction of one person's time, that stays on top of current project performance, brings project issues to the surface, and presents the "state of the project union" to the executive team? (See Chapter 4.)

- Through what process will projects be added to the portfolio? What process will cause projects to be delayed or cancelled?

- How will you ensure that the culture reinforces optimum project performance? (See Chapter 5.)

- How will you ensure that project sponsors, managers, and team members have the skills necessary to carry out their roles? (See Chapter 6.)

- How will you ensure that people issues are addressed in projects?

Like any business process, the steps in project portfolio management should be mapped. While the phases we are presenting can serve as the high-level framework for any organization, the what and when of the detailed steps in each phase need to be customized to your situation. The who—the roles, covered in Chapter 6—needs to be clearly established. And, the project-portfolio-management process needs to be linked to other processes with which it interfaces, including the product development/launch process, the budgeting process, and the performance management/appraisal process.

Our consumer goods human resources department found that the most valuable outgrowth of its OPP project was not the initial prioritization exercise, but the ongoing strengthening of its relationships with and reputation among its internal customers. Because the "voice of the customer" was loud and clear throughout department deliberations, the process aligned HR projects with customer priorities. For the first time, customers perceived this department as being focused on their needs and not on pursuits that were driven by HR's parochial interests and perceptions of "what's good for them." The department installed an ongoing process for reporting on initiative status to its customers and involved them in formal updates to the project portfolio.

As fulfilling as the Customtravel executive team members found the "go now/go later/no go" decision making, they recognized that this process would yield its maximum return only if it became baked into the ongoing management of the business. Specifically, they

- *Established a standing executive committee agenda item in which they would review the status of the six core strategy-implementation initiatives.*

- *Initiated a process in which each line of business and department would go through the same Optimum Project Portfolio process that they had just completed at the corporate level.*

- *Established a protocol and template for recommending the launch of any project that would consume more than 100 person-hours.*

- *Established a one-person project office that would keep its finger on the pulse of project activity.*

- *Initiated a study of those aspects of the culture that either supported or failed to support project excellence.*

OPP Step 5 goes well beyond establishing an Optimum Project Portfolio. This process addresses all of the critical success factors displayed in Figure 3-1, including those covered in the chapters that follow. It serves as the foundation of strategy implementation.

CREATING AN OPTIMAL PROJECT PORTFOLIO: A CASE STUDY

During its strategy-formulation process, the top team of a U.S.-based multinational consumer products company had a blinding insight. This "old-economy" company concluded that its primary competitive advantages were the strength of its brand and its ability to facilitate customer-to-customer communication. As the team members brainstormed ways to leverage these strengths, they identified an opportunity to offer a digital service, delivered via the 2.5G and 3G mobile phones that were becoming *de rigueur* in Europe and Southeast Asia. Because they were concerned that this opportunity would be stifled in their legacy environment, they set up a separate company to pursue it. The corporation was to play the role of venture capitalist, providing funding and monitoring progress, but not installing onerous controls or imposing its "analog culture."

Having facilitated the team's strategy deliberations, we were asked to help identify, prioritize, plan, and support the delivery of the projects needed to build this new business. We began by using the Enterprise Model, displayed in Chapters 1 and 2, to identify the projects. After some whittling, combining, and a raised voice or two, the executive team's list contained 30 strategic initiatives, grouped into seven programs.

Because the business had an initial compliment of 25 people, it could not start all 30 projects at the same time. So, the top team confronted the two questions that anchor this chapter:

• How many projects can we take on?

• How can we be sure that we launch the projects that will contribute most to the implementation of the strategy?

In OPP Step 1, the team used its newly forged strategy as the basis for developing screening and priority-setting criteria (see Figure 3-2).

We and the team were pleased with the balance that the criteria struck between short-term and long-term needs, external and internal focus, and blue-sky entrepreneurship and feet-on-the-ground business sense.

The team quickly realized that the criteria were not equally important. The numbers that appear in parentheses in Figure 3-2 reflect the relative weight of each criterion in the priority setting.

As this was a small start-up operation that was dedicated 100 percent to projects, it was relatively easy to determine

FIGURE 3-2   The Relationship between Strategic Imperatives and Project-Prioritization Criteria in a Digital Services Company

Strategic Imperatives	Project Prioritization Criteria
The Opportunity	
Rapidly growing base of wireless consumers	Maximize speed to market (10)
Immature competition	
Consumers able and willing to pay for personalized, fun 2.5G- & 3G-based services	
The Proposition	Support the delivery of the strategic proposition (9)
Target young consumers where wireless penetration is greatest	
Use parent's global brand strengths to gain market & benefit consumers	Support use of parent brand (5)
Value Generation	
Adhere to a budget for IT build, salary, overhead, and marketing costs	Maximize return on investment (8)
Aim to break even in three years	
Manage business risk associated with building on rapidly evolving technology	Minimize business risk (5)
Successful implementation of first phase will require	Maximize value to external partners (7)
Multiple strong partnerships	
Getting the right resources in the right place quickly	Minimize time to recruit and deploy the right employees (7)
Strong IT platform	Support robust process & IT development (4)

project capacity (OPP Step 2) and current project load (Step 3). Because the company didn't yet have a formal organization structure, we identified the average number of days available for project pursuits in each core skill set, such as business development, research, and finance.

In OPP Step 4, members of the senior team went through a rigorous decision-making process in which each project was compared to the other 29 on each criterion. Then they factored in the weights, ensuring that the project that was strongest in "maximize speed to market" had twice as much clout as the one that did best in "support utilization of parent brand." While they did not eliminate any projects during this process, they were able to slot each project into one of four "priority quartiles." This hierarchy guided both resource allocation and sequence. For example, the "organization structure development" project was in the same priority quartile as, but was dependent on and therefore needed to follow, the "sales and account management process design" project.

Armed with priority and sequence, the team members moved to establish the schedule. They used their capacity analysis—the output of OPP Steps 2 and 3—to determine how much of this work they could take on at any one time. For example, they determined that the sixth project out of the gate ("brand guidelines developed") exhausted their marketing resources. Other initiatives requiring marketing expertise were scheduled after those skills had been freed up. The full set of projects was scheduled over 16 months.

The top team understood that project portfolio creation couldn't be a "one-off" effort. As described in Step 5, it put in place a process for the ongoing review and update of its project portfolio and an infrastructure for supporting project excellence.

The top team found the OPP rigor to be challenging but worthwhile. Going through the process brought to the surface issues and decisions that in all likelihood would not otherwise have become visible. And, more importantly, the top team felt that it had a game plan for strategy implementation and a business that was under control.

This example is for an entire, albeit small, business. In large organizations, we frequently find that creating an OPP should be done at the department and division level, as well as the corporate level.

A WORD ON FOCUS

At first blush, the Optimal Project Portfolio process may appear to be a bit formulaic. But if you are like other executives with whom we have worked, you should fully internalize the process after one iteration. While it does crunch hour and dollar numbers, the process is rooted in the understanding that the hallmark of an effective organization is *focus*. In today's fiercely competitive marketplace, even an organization with deep pockets must conserve its human and financial resources.

Think about it:

> How many balls can you keep in the air? Would you rather implement nine projects with acceptable results or three projects with spectacular results?

Managing your project portfolio is like managing the assets in your investment portfolio. Your portfolio is unique to your situation. It must align your funds with your needs. It must be monitored. It needs to be adjusted regularly to fit new circumstances.

Subsequent chapters describe the infrastructure that you can put in place and practices that you can employ to ensure that your project portfolio supports the implementation of your strategy and meets your expectations for return on investment.

4

STRUCTURING FOR STRATEGIC SUCCESS

GWEN PHILIPS IS EXECUTIVE VICE PRESIDENT OF OPERATIONS for Wichita One, a regional retail bank with $1 billion in assets. She is proud of her company's growth, profitability, customer retention, and freedom from the questionable business practices that have plagued some of Wichita's larger rivals. From its modest perch in the midwestern United States, it has had a significant influence on the industry, particularly in the use of technology and the development of services for middle-income customers.

Gwen and her colleagues on the leadership team believe that Wichita's success is largely the result of two assets: a culture that fosters innovation and an ability to efficiently bring breakthrough ideas to fruition. During their most recent strategy update, the team members evaluated a number of alternative directions and decided to remain on the same path. For the first time, they formally stated that the development of new services will be the company's primary competitive advantage and will serve as its principal source of growth.

Never satisfied with the status quo, Gwen believes that there are some chinks in Wichita's service development armor:

- *Its core competence is to a large degree the result of the skills of the small number of people who routinely manage new venture projects. While she is pleased to have that talent on board, she thinks it's risky for Wichita to rely on individual heroics. The project managers appear to be loyal to the company, but she doesn't want the company's long-term health to be so dependent on the retention of a handful of gifted individuals.*

- *She is concerned about executive involvement. She believes that she and her peers on the executive team are not sufficiently informed about or involved in initiative creation and definition. She is sure that initiatives would benefit from their guidance and from their industry and company perspective, which is broader than that of lower-level people. And, once strategic initiatives are defined, she thinks that the team should be closer to the status of their deployment. After all, these projects are nothing less than the fuel for the fire of Wichita's competitive advantage.*

- *As the number, complexity, and significance of initiatives increases, Gwen foresees a future in which projects bump into one another, compete for resources in ways that are not healthy, and fail to achieve cross-project synergies. While Gwen does not want to dim the entrepreneurial light of the project managers, she would like to see more coordination of their efforts.*

- *Another coordination gap lies in the interfaces between projects and the ongoing operations of the bank. For example, the team charged with developing new services for high-net-worth individuals is insufficiently linked to, and increasingly experiencing tension with, the relationship management and trust departments.*

A cornerstone of Wichita's success is its ability to execute. Gwen thinks that closing these gaps could put it even further ahead of the pack.

FIGURE 4-1   Initiative Organization Structure: A Critical Success Factor for Strategy Implementation

ALIGNING INITIATIVE STRUCTURE
WITH TRADITIONAL STRUCTURE

"If we can just get the right organization structure and the right person heading up each department, all of our problems will evaporate." While no executive would agree with this statement, too many behave as if this were their mantra. The investment in most reorganizations exceeds the return, and with good reason. Too many executives routinely throw structural solutions at problems that are not caused by a flaw in the configuration of boxes on the organization chart.

Take this common scenario: A managing director is disappointed with the number of successful new products emerging from his company's pipeline. He responds by reorganizing the research and development and marketing departments and replacing the heads of these departments. However, no matter how elegant the structure and how dazzling the new leaders, these actions will not fully address the deficiency—and may even exacerbate it—if its roots are embedded in a deficient product development process, a culture that squelches innovation, or a dearth of systems-engineering talent. Because reorganizations are wrenching, productivity-sapping events, we want to reserve that medication for situations in which we're sure it will cure the disease.

While we do not want to ascribe to structure more healing powers than it merits, it is one of the variables that influence the successful implementation of strategic initiatives (see Figure 4-1). The contribution of talented project sponsors, managers, and team members may be lessened if the structure is an impediment to getting the job done. Every minute that they spend working around or doing battle with the structure is a minute that is not dedicated to more productive pursuits. Structures channel behavior. An unsupportive structure can make necessary relationships difficult to forge, necessary commitment difficult to build, and necessary authority difficult to exercise.

Because initiatives are your strategy implementation vehicles, you don't want the structure to be nails in the road. We recommend that you begin by determining the elements of your existing structure that support optimum project performance and those that compromise effectiveness or speed. Then, and only then, make the changes necessary to remove the unhealthy tissue. Your challenge is to select a structure that enables initiatives to flourish without compromising the ongoing business.

SELECTING AN INITIATIVE-SUPPORTIVE STRUCTURE

To align your organization structure squarely behind both strategic projects and day-to-day operations, we suggest that you and your executive colleagues follow a three-step process:

STEP 1: DEFINE THE STRUCTURE-SELECTION CRITERIA

These criteria are the characteristics of an organization structure that serves the needs of both initiatives and ongoing operations. They will serve as the framework within which alternative structures will do battle in Step 3.

Gwen Philips, the Wichita One executive vice president who opens this chapter, convinced her colleagues that the highly skilled individuals who populated the bank's new venture initiative teams needed to be supported by the bank's structure. The team members began by establishing their criteria:

- *Maximize the effectiveness of key strategic and tactical initiatives.*

- *Maximize the efficiency of key initiatives.*

- *Optimize executive involvement in guiding key initiatives.*

- *Minimize negative impact on ongoing operational processes.*

- *Motivate employees.*

- *Maximize role clarity.*

- *Minimize the time and cost of implementing changes.*

They considered assigning weights to these objectives to indicate their relative importance, but they did not do so because they concluded that each should exert the same influence on their decision.

STEP 2: GENERATE ALTERNATIVE STRUCTURES

Because you want to consider a broad spectrum of options, this step puts a premium on creativity. Flawed as it may be, the current structure should always be included; although imperfect, it may carry no more baggage than other alternatives. Doing nothing is sometimes the best choice.

The alternatives should be described at a level of detail that enables them to be assessed against the criteria developed in Step 1.

The Wichita One team developed these alternatives:

- *Alternative A: Maintain the current structure and roles, in which project managers and team members have both initiative responsibilities and functional responsibilities.*

- *Alternative B: For significant (term to be defined) initiatives, designate full-time project managers and team members and have them report to the existing functional heads, who will continue to serve as sponsors.*

- *Alternative C: Designate full-time project managers and team members and have them report to a newly formed "Project Office" that will take responsibility for project performance.*

- *Alternative D: Alternative A plus a Project Office staffed by two full-time project management experts, who would not formally supervise project managers, as in Alternative C, but would guide, facilitate, provide tools, and report on all significant changes.*

- *Alternative E: Full-time project managers and team members as described in Alternative B plus the Project Office outlined in Alternative D.*

STEP 3: EVALUATE THE ALTERNATIVES
AND SELECT THE BEST STRUCTURE

Since there is no universally correct way to integrate initiatives and functional activities, this step's purpose is to determine the project structure that best meets the organization's needs at a particular point in time. Each alternative is compared to the others in terms of each criterion. For example, how does each alternative fare in terms of initiative efficiency? What are the implications of each for ongoing (nonproject) operations? When this step is carried out rigorously, it stimulates a robust discussion of the strengths and weaknesses of each structure and often results in the generation of new alternatives.

The Wichita One team members used their Step 1 criteria to test the relative strength of each of the five alternative structures that were identified in Step 2. They determined that Alternatives D and E, while not the strongest on every criterion, met the entire set of criteria better than the three others. After assessing the risks associated with these two alternatives, they selected Alternative E.

WHAT IS A PROJECT OFFICE AND WHY IS IT USEFUL?

As you reviewed the alternatives considered by Wichita One, you may have been intrigued by the concept of a Project Office. To begin exploring this structural alternative, let's examine some analogies:

- A CEO is responsible for the strategy of the business. However, he or she may have a strategic planning officer who coordinates the collecting and organizing of strategic intelligence, the planning calendar, strategy meetings, and the reporting of progress in strategy implementation.

- A plant manager is responsible for safety at his or her site. However, he or she typically has a safety officer who collects and disseminates performance information, guides the safety issue resolution process, serves as the repository of safety policies, identifies the need for and coordinates safety training, and serves as the "staff conscience" of a safe working environment.

- A vice president of operations is responsible for product quality, but she or he may have a full- or part-time quality officer who plays the same five roles as the safety officer.

Given the criticality and resource consumption of initiatives, many organizations have set up Project Offices that play a role similar to the strategy, safety, and quality offices. The Project Office serves as "mission control" for all of the projects that are underway, are about to be launched, and are being proposed. Just as with the strategic planning, safety, and quality offices, the Project Office's responsibilities may be shouldered by a person with other duties, a person who does nothing else, or—in a project-intensive organization—two or three people.

The objective of this function is not to take responsibility for the performance of individual projects. If it bureaucratizes initiative deployment, it has failed. A good human resources function improves the way line managers care for and develop people; it doesn't manage people for them. A strong finance department improves line managers' financial stewardship and provides them with information upon which to base decisions; it doesn't manage the numbers for them. Similarly, a robust Project Office can more than pay for itself by improving the project performance of the executive team, sponsors, project managers, and team members.

Our objective is not to sell you on setting up a Project Office, but to help you understand it well enough to consider its potential value.

WHAT DOES A PROJECT OFFICE DO?

The Project Office needs to be custom-designed to meet the unique needs of the organization's project workload and environment. Its members typically play some or all of these roles:

- Own the *Project Proposal process* (see Chapter 2). A Project Office creates an effective, efficient format for pitching initiatives and designs a process in which the appropriate individual or group provides a prompt, reasoned decision on the recommendation. It also ensures that the process includes evaluation/screening criteria. It often helps project initiators define and collect the information—for example, resource requirement estimates—that enables executives to pass judgment on the recommendation.

- Own the *Optimum Project Portfolio process*, in which the overall project complement is assessed for priority and manageability, as we discussed in Chapter 3. This process includes realigning the portfolio when a new project is launched, a project is completed, priorities change, or project resource consumption is greater or less

than planned. The executive team is the portfolio decision-making body; the Project Office instigates the decisions, frames the decisions, documents the decisions, and
ensures that the decisions are carried out.

- Assess the *health of the initiative environment* and serve as
the focal point for identifying and removing obstacles to
first-class project performance (see Chapter 5). For example, during its strategy deliberations, the top team of an
insurance company decided to forge an alliance with a
brokerage firm that could manage the investment element of its growing annuity business. The company's
one-person Project Office was the first to see that this
critical initiative was floundering. She identified the
cause as being rooted in a cultural characteristic: extreme
aversion to risk. She presented her analysis to the executive team, facilitated its decision making and action planning, and oversaw the implementation of the steps that it
decided to take to remove the cultural impediments.
   A Project Office may also be responsible for managing the information that feeds the project dimension of
an organization's performance appraisal/management
system.

- Ensure that the organization understands the what, why,
and how of the *roles*—sponsor, project manager, team
member, target population—that are played in successful
initiatives (see Chapter 6).

- Spearhead the selection and installation of a *common language* for project/initiative management. This language
includes processes, templates, and software (see Chapter
7 and Appendix A). Project Office staff upgrade the
methodology when better tools become available. They
customize the techniques for the organization environment. They provide tools and training to initiative contributors. And they troubleshoot projects that go off the
rails.

- *Monitor* the organization's overall project performance
in terms of results, cost, and time, and report on that

performance to the executive team (see Chapter 8). This role does not usurp that of the project manager or project sponsor. While these individuals are responsible for monitoring and reporting on their individual projects, the project officer reports on the performance of the entire project portfolio. The use of visual signals— such as red, yellow, and green lights to signify project status—can enable executives to quickly review the health of individual initiatives and the overall project landscape.

- *Establish and streamline the interfaces* between initiatives. In this role, the goals that the Project Office should pursue include the following:
  - *Share information, learning, and deliverables.* For example, an inventory management improvement project and a wireless local-area network project that involve the same people should work hand in glove. We worked with a durable goods company in which one of the Project Office's key roles was coordinating the outputs of two process-improvement teams, one of which was focused on order fulfillment and the other on manufacturing.
  - *Ensure that the same philosophy is guiding project activities.* For example, a strategic commitment to outsourcing noncore functions should be driving both a logistics-streamlining project and a back-office staff rationalization project.
  - *Establish an appropriate initiative sequence.* For example, a strategy formulation project should precede a project to develop a marketing program.
  - *Avoid overlaps.* For example, a help desk enhancement project championed by Customer Service and a customer care training project spearheaded by Human Resources could easily end up addressing the same needs and even taking the same actions. Worse, they could develop solutions that pursue a common goal in different ways, squandering resources and reducing focus.

- *Avoid "underlaps,"* in which two projects are each proceeding on the assumption that a deliverable is being produced by the other. For example, a bank's investment planning product team and its premium client marketing team may each be assuming that the other is developing asset-allocation templates.
- *Address interproject conflicts and synergies.* Because the Project Office has the aerial view of the entire project landscape, it is in the best position to see and address conflicts. For example, a product launch should not be butting heads with a cost-reduction initiative.
- *Ensure that potential opportunities* ("1 + 1 = 3s") are identified and realized. For example, a plant may benefit exponentially by forging strong links between a maintenance improvement project and an equipment upgrade project. (For a discussion of Potential Opportunity Analysis, see Appendix A.)

- Capture and disseminate *lessons learned* so that future projects can
  - Draw on the framework established by the project. For example, the work breakdown structure of an order fulfillment improvement project may be an effective template—or at least a point of departure—for other business process improvement projects.
  - Repeat and extend the benefits of what went well. For example, a project manager may have done a particularly effective and timely job of reallocating resources to meet new demands, a frequent need in almost all projects.
  - Avoid the aspects of a project that didn't go well. For example, a project may serve as the poster child for how not to communicate to and solicit input from stakeholders.
  - Benefit from prior projects in a certain area (e.g., the fiber products division), with a certain target population (e.g., researchers), or with a certain sponsor (e.g., the vice president of engineering).

When the volume of project history information reaches critical mass, the Project Office may create a database with keyword search capability, enabling interested parties to access lessons-learned information directly.

THE PROJECT OFFICE: A MEANS OR AN END? PERMANENT OR TEMPORARY?

The purpose of a Project Office is to provide project-process ownership, project control, graduate-level initiative management skills, facilitation, project reporting, and an information clearinghouse. If you can meet those needs without adding a separate box on the organization chart, great.

An organization that has embedded quality into its processes and practices may no longer need a quality department. In effect, everybody is in the quality department. Similarly, an organization may reach a level of project maturity that makes a Project Office superfluous. However, project excellence demands that some individual or group assume the roles just described. And, those roles should be assigned at the beginning of an initiative rather than after it has hit the shoals.

WHO SHOULD STAFF THE PROJECT OFFICE?

A Project Office—regardless of whether it is staffed with several full-time people or one part-timer—should contain one or more individuals with

- Extensive and varied project management experience

- A mastery of the project management process that has been adopted as a common language (see Chapter 7)

- The ability to facilitate teams

- Credibility with and access to the executives who serve as initiative sponsors

- Credibility with project managers and team members

- Compulsive attention to detail

- The ability to juggle multiple balls (or, more typically, a ball, a tennis racket, an anvil, and a burning torch)

In an increasing percentage of our strategy clients, in addition to or instead of setting up a Project Office, the CEO appoints a strategy implementation officer. This individual—who may be full- or part-time—coordinates and champions the execution of all strategic initiatives. This person plays a Project Office role, at least for the strategy elements of the project portfolio.

WHAT IS THE DOWNSIDE OF SETTING UP A PROJECT OFFICE?

Like any other investment, a Project Office is not without risks and sacrifices. For example, it requires the time of one or more talented individuals. If it is mismanaged or poorly supervised, it can degenerate into an unwelcome and constraining policing function. It can retard and bureaucratize rather than facilitate and streamline. And, it can devolve into a toothless staff function populated by out-to-pasture resources.

A Potential Problem Analysis (see Appendix A) can help you take the actions necessary to avoid these pitfalls.

WHAT ELSE CAN YOU DO TO CREATE A STRUCTURE THAT SUPPORTS INITIATIVES?

A Project Office is not the only structural arrow in your strategy implementation quiver. Regardless of whether you create a Project Office, you should scour your structure for other opportunities to support initiatives. For example, we guided the team charged with improving a computer manufacturer's product development process. During that project, the team made structural changes that broke down the functional "silos" that were impeding the performance of new-product initiatives. In another instance, we helped a niche defense contractor establish engineering "centers of excellence" that facilitated access to the individuals whose skills were necessary for project success.

ALIGNING THE ORGANIZATION STRUCTURE: A CASE STUDY

The top team of a pharmaceutical company was increasingly worried about the pace of strategy implementation. The team had invested a considerable amount of time in modifying the company's product emphasis and identifying new markets. Its members realized that changes of this magnitude weren't going to happen overnight; however, they were beginning to wonder if they would happen in their lifetime.

The company had become fairly skilled at identifying sponsors, project managers, and team members for strategic initiatives. However, the executives suspected that the organization's structure was impeding the efforts of these talented, hard-working individuals. They asked us to conduct an independent analysis of the situation. The conclusions:

- The existing organization was characterized by strong, isolated, and competitive departments whose managers consigned cross-functional projects to orphan status. As a result, (1) potential sponsors perceived organization-wide initiatives as a distraction from their primary mission, and (2) it was difficult to free up talented resources to serve as project managers and team members.

- Once projects were launched, there were no clear guidelines that helped people strike the right balance between completing their project work and fulfilling their functional responsibilities. The informal reward system consistently drove people toward their "day job," causing their project contributions to suffer.

- There was no forum for commissioning new projects, modifying existing projects, or debating and resolving project issues. Change-program reviews were limited to a standing 30-minute agenda item at monthly executive committee meetings. These time slots were insufficient for executive education, commitment building, and direction setting. In addition, the limited energy that the executives devoted to these initiatives sent an unintentional but clear signal that the initiatives were not a high priority.

This company was making good progress in establishing project roles. It was also institutionalizing sound project management processes and tools. However, the analysis led the executive team to conclude that these actions were not enough. The team's initiative performance concerns could be addressed only if it arrived at the right answer to the question that anchors this chapter:

> How, if at all, should the existing organization structure be modified or changed to optimize strategic and other mission-critical initiatives without compromising ongoing operations?

To ensure calibration within the executive team and to establish the basis for structure selection, the team established these criteria:

- Motivate employees.
- Maximize the clarity of both initiatives and functional roles.
- Promote effective and timely project decision making.
- Facilitate effective project and functional management.
- Minimize time to deliver project benefits.
- Minimize disruption caused by changes.
- Minimize implementation time.

We then helped the team develop a set of alternative structures:

- *Alternative A: Stay as we are.* The current functional structure is left unchanged. The five directors—operations, sales and marketing, finance, human resources, and legal and property—will serve as initiative sponsors. Sponsors will select project managers within their functions. The sponsor and manager will jointly select a cross-functional project team. For projects that are grouped together in a program, the function head with the most at stake will serve as the program director, coordinating activities and running interference across projects.

- *Alternative B: Have full-time project teams with line-management project directors.* As in Alternative A, the functional directors will serve as sponsors. However, project managers will be line managers who report directly to the directors. Project team members will continue to report on a solid-line basis to their departments, but they will be dedicated full-time to critical projects and return to their function upon project completion. They will have a dotted-line relationship with project managers. When the organization lacks needed skills, team members will be recruited from outside the company and deployed to the appropriate function upon project completion. Program directors hold the same positions and play the same role as in Alternative A.

- *Alternative C: Have autonomous project groups.* Unlike in Alternative B, the reporting relationships of the full-time project managers and team members will change. They will report on a solid-line basis to newly formed project organizations. For megaprojects, sponsors will be full-time. Program directors will dedicate a larger percentage of their time to their project responsibilities and will be expected to be more immersed in project status and activities than in Alternatives A and B.

- *Alternative D: Matrix.* Project managers will be dedicated full-time to their projects, but team members will not. The percentage of members' time that will be devoted to projects will be negotiated when initiatives are defined. Rather than simply adding projects to the full plates of the organization's most valuable individuals, functional roles will be redesigned to accommodate project responsibilities. Sponsor and program director positions and responsibilities will be the same as in Alternative C.

The executive team evaluated each of these alternatives against the criteria. Given the importance of this decision and the fact that there was no obvious winner, the executives documented their thinking in a decision matrix. Some of their conclusions were

- Alternative C was strongest in "maximize clarity of both initiative and functional roles" and "minimize time to deliver project benefits." However, it tied with Alternative D as the weakest in terms of "minimize disruption" and "minimize implementation time."

- Alternative D fared best in terms of "motivate employees," "promote effective and timely project decision making," and "facilitate effective project and functional management."

- Alternative B wasn't the strongest in terms of any of the objectives and was tied for last place in "promote effective and timely project decision making" and "facilitate effective project and functional management."

- Because it represented no change, Alternative A was the strongest in "minimize disruption" and "minimize implementation time." However, it was the weakest or tied for the weakest in terms of all the other objectives.

Based on this analysis, the executives selected the matrix structure provided by Alternative D. They were particularly attracted to the separation of project and functional decision making, which guarantees focus on strategic initiatives. By staffing initiatives with people who "went home" to their departments between project activities, this alternative ensured that changes designed by project teams considered the real-world upsides and downsides of implementation.

They created a centralized Project Office that they called the Program Management Office. This function was assigned the responsibility for strategic alignment, cross-project integration, methods, skills, issue resolution, monitoring, reporting, and knowledge management across the operations function for all projects budgeted at greater than $125,000. It was staffed with three full-time project-management experts. They also set up local Project Offices that played the same roles within each division. These functions each had two full-time project-management experts.

Before committing to this alternative, the executive team conducted a risk analysis. The most significant potential problem they identified was rooted in the traditional baggage of all matrix structures: people being torn between the competing demands of their solid- and dotted-line bosses. In addition to the role adjustment described earlier, they set up a consequence-free channel for initiative team members to bring up any concerns they had in this area.

COMMENT

No structure can compensate for weaknesses in project sponsorship, management, methodology, and culture. However, a structure that is strategically aligned enables talented individuals to realize their potential and draws attention to shortcomings in skills, tools, and environment. It serves as one of the load-bearing pillars under initiative excellence.

5

CREATING A
CAN-DO CULTURE

*T*HE LEADERSHIP AT SAYBROOK AVIATION, *which manages private plane terminals at a variety of small-market airports, has articulated a strategy in which its growth engine will be a broader set of services offered to current customers. In addition to basic aircraft storage and flight services, Saybrook will offer routine maintenance, route planning, overnight accommodations, carry-aboard meals, and pilot training. The company recognizes the importance of initiative management in transforming that vision into reality.*

Using the new company strategy as a beacon, the members of the top team identified potential initiatives (see Chapter 2). They winnowed their project candidates to a manageable number that reflected the organization's highest priorities (see Chapter 3). They created a Project Office and built cross-functional processes that broke down some of the functional silos that impeded project success (see Chapter 4). They trained people to play various project roles and to use a robust, consistent approach to project management (see Chapters 6 and 7).

Initiative Nirvana? Not yet. In spite of establishing the underpinnings of initiative success, performance is lackluster. Projects routinely go over budget. They frequently meet their schedules only by pulling valuable resources from other initiatives and forcing people to work around the clock. When people sniff a project approaching, they hide.

A cause analysis revealed that Saybrook's deficiency is not in initiative structure or process. Nor is it in skills. It is rooted in a dimension of strategy implementation that the top team has not addressed: culture. The organization's culture is, for the most part, healthy; however, it has never been aligned with initiative success. Cultural characteristics in areas such as communication, feedback, and reward systems do not just inadequately consider initiative excellence, they actually work against it.

WHAT IS "CULTURE"?

Culture is the prevailing norms, beliefs, values, and practices that make up the personality of an organization. Its characteristics include everything from the way in which customers are treated, to the degree to which employees trust one another, to whether meetings start on time, to the tone of e-mails, to the balance that people strike between their work and their personal lives.

Think of culture as a gravitational force that has a profound influence on decision making and behavior (see Figure 5-1). In most companies, that force remains hidden and is perceived—incorrectly—as impervious to change.

There are many influences on culture. One is the nature of an organization's customers. Wal-Mart suppliers adopt aspects of the Wal-Mart culture. Defense contractors tend to mirror the military culture. Pharmaceutical companies look and sound a lot like doctors. Culture is also affected by the values of the founders, even after they are gone. Consider the lasting impact of Walt Disney, McDonald's Ray Kroc, and Hallmark's Joyce Hall. Organizations' focal jobs also mold the culture. Hewlett-Packard has an engineering culture. Procter & Gamble has a marketing culture. General Motors stumbled when bean counters wrested power from the "car guys" and put their imprint on the culture. An organization's location can also guide its conduct, even in global corporations. Japanese companies tend to have different norms and mores from American and German companies. Companies based in the rural South look and feel different from those with a center of gravity in the urban North.

However, all of these influences pale in comparison with the dominant force propelling an organization's culture: executive behavior. Your values, priorities, personality, and ways of interacting with people shape practices throughout your organization. A key dimension of your top management role is to define and install the culture that best supports your strategy.

FIGURE 5-1   Initiative Culture: A Critical Success Factor for Strategy Implementation

Culture change does not happen overnight, but cultures can—and often need to—change. Just look at the ways in which Sandy Weill transformed the Citibank culture, Lou Gerstner revolutionized the environment of IBM, and Steve Jobs invigorated Apple when he returned. And both supporters and detractors acknowledge the impact that Roger Smith had on the culture of GM and Michael Eisner on Disney. And, as we write, GE CEO Jeffrey Immelt is making changes to the much-praised culture installed by his predecessor, Jack Welch. He is putting more emphasis on sales growth through customer-driven innovation and a bit less on process-driven cost reduction. Toward that end, he has launched strategic initiatives that focus on changing the reward system, increasing the funding and influence of marketing, and hiring industry experts from outside GE. His reasons are not rooted in dysfunctionality in the legacy culture, but rather in changes in the economic and competitive landscape.

If you work for a large organization, your corporate culture is most likely a melting pot of subcultures. If you have grown through acquisitions, there are most likely differences in the legacy cultures of the original company and the acquired companies. Even if your company has not made acquisitions, your various divisions, departments, and geographic locations probably have distinct cultures. That's not necessarily undesirable. While you should have a set of shared values across the corporation, you may want your wholesale and retail divisions, your marketing and finance departments, your Japanese and Australian operations, and your regulated and unregulated businesses to have unique attributes and practices.

Cultural differences can be a source of energizing strength, and even of competitive advantage. However, when cultural differences boil over into cultural clashes, you're headed for trouble. It's tough to implement strategy in a house divided.

Figure 5-2 reintroduces the Enterprise Model that we have used to position the various components of strategy implementation. As you can see, culture is a critical element supporting both the strategic and the operational dimensions of

FIGURE 5-2 Culture's Position in an Enterprise

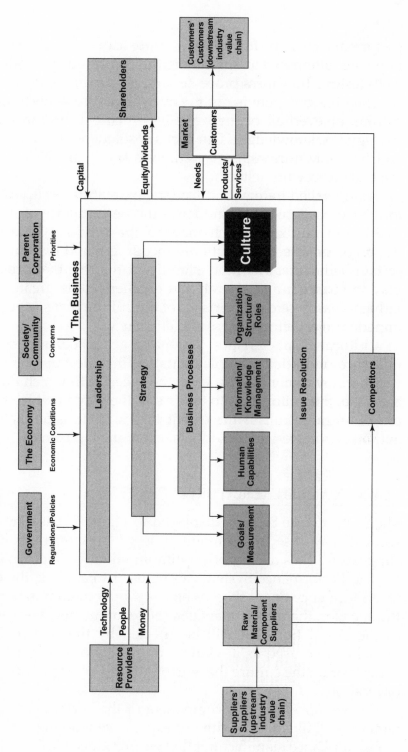

performance. A dysfunctional culture can cripple strategy implementation by suboptimizing the contributions made by well-designed business processes and talented people.

The objective here is not to cover the entire waterfront of culture, or even all of the ways in which culture can affect strategy implementation. Our focus is solely on the degree to which your culture supports initiatives and your role in shaping that culture.

Along with strategy and leadership, culture occupies the top tier of variables that influence the performance of initiatives. Your culture—which may be the product of careful design or unfettered evolution—encourages and discourages certain behaviors. The more significant the role that projects play in strategic and operational excellence, the greater the influence of those characteristics of the culture that support or impede project effectiveness and efficiency.

Cultural characteristics that have a particularly strong influence on initiative implementation include the degree to which innovation is encouraged, the speed with which things are done, the willingness to take risks, the way in which people communicate, and the extent to which decision-making authority is vested in individuals below the top team.

HOW CAN A CULTURE SUPPORT PROJECTS?

The Performance System, displayed in Figure 5-3, is a framework that we use to examine the degree to which a culture supports (or fails to support) optimum initiative deployment.

The Performance System can be used to analyze the culture's influence on all those who contribute to an initiative—the sponsor, the project manager, the team members—as well as the population that will be affected by the change. The model can be used as a window on the "project culture" in general or on the culture that surrounds a specific project type or location.

As we introduce each component of the Performance System, we will illustrate it with our experience working with the global appliance manufacturer that we introduced in Chapter 2.

FIGURE 5-3   The Performance System

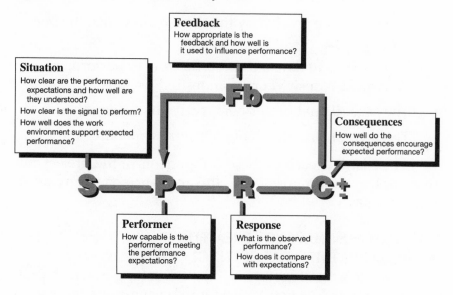

THE RESPONSE: WHAT BEHAVIORS ARE YOU LOOKING FOR?

The *response* is the set of results and behaviors that are expected from each project contributor. For example, the primary desired response of a project manager is the on-time, within-budget delivery of a project that meets its performance standards. Other responses might include effective leadership of project meetings, frequent status reporting to the initiative sponsor, and appropriate solicitation of input from the target population. To ensure clarity of expectations, the sponsor and the project manager would have to define "effective," "frequent," and "appropriate."

The appliance manufacturer's executives were concerned that their strategic initiatives were not being implemented quickly enough. Although each project had been carefully prioritized, resourced, and planned, the top team concluded that those responsible for delivery were too focused on their "day job" to devote the necessary time and attention to projects. The executives defined their desired response for project managers and team members as: without sacrificing ongoing operations, devote the time and energy necessary to ensure that strategic initiatives achieve their objectives on time and on budget.

The quality and timeliness of a response are a function of

- The support provided by the *situation* in which the performers must make the response

- The positive and negative *consequences* to performers who make a desired or an undesired response

- The *feedback* that performers receive on their response

- The breadth and depth of *performers'* capabilities

Let's examine each of these components of the project culture engine, continuing to use the appliance company as an illustration. ·

THE SITUATION: HAVE YOU CREATED
A SUPPORTIVE INITIATIVE SETTING?

A critical element of culture is the work setting in which project contributors function. Consider these questions about each performer's situation:

> Are the project roles and expectations clear and achievable?

For example,

- Do sponsors and project managers understand both the task management and people management dimensions of their roles? Are they assessed against appropriate metrics?

- Do team members who are not dedicated full-time to projects understand how they are to balance their project and their day-job responsibilities? Are they assessed against appropriate metrics?

- Are expectations adjusted when necessary to reflect changes in the external environment, the progress of the initiative, the lessons learned from the initiative, and the resources dedicated to the initiative?

Are project processes and protocols logical?

For example,

- Are projects well defined (in terms of overall intent, specific objectives, a breakdown of the work to be performed, and resource requirements)?

- Are projects well planned (including the sequencing and scheduling of steps, the assignment and scheduling of responsibilities, and protection against risks to the plan)?

- Is the project implementation process (monitoring, modifying, and closeout) effective and efficient?

(See Appendix A for definitions and examples of each of the steps in parentheses.)

Do project contributors have access to the information they need in order to do their work?
Does the project have adequate resources (time, people, money, tools, and equipment)?
Is the physical work setting conducive to project excellence?

For example, do team members have sufficient privacy, a manageable number of interruptions, and a "war room" in which to post their work?

Each question with a no answer is an area in which people have to swim against the current to make their initiative contribution.

At the appliance manufacturer, most components of the situation section of the initiative performance engine were running smoothly. Through the Optimal Project Portfolio process (see Chapter 3), the executive team had established appropriate project priorities and adequately funded strategic initiatives. Processes and protocols were codified. Sponsor, project manager, and team member roles had been defined. Necessary information was readily available. The work setting was conducive to project work.

However, one piece of "dirt in the engine" concerned expectations. The executive team had not forcefully communicated the priority of strategic initiatives. It did not adequately measure project performance. It had not sufficiently defined the balance it wanted initiative contributors to strike between their ongoing responsibilities and responsibilities for projects. As a matter of fact, the team had unwittingly sent signals that people should work on initiatives "in their spare time."

To address this Performance System weakness, the top team issued a directive that described the importance of initiatives to the company's future. Its members reinforced that message in every presentation they gave and every meeting they attended. To ensure that initiatives were carried out by the committed rather than the conscripted, they invited volunteers from all functions and levels to apply for project responsibilities. They were pleased to see that these positions were heavily oversubscribed; they saw the sign-up rate as an indicator that people throughout the organization shared their passion for substantive change.

CONSEQUENCES: ARE YOU REWARDING INITIATIVE EXCELLENCE?
A critical project-success variable is the consequence system within which all project contributors must perform. Because of its complexity and power, let's explore the consequences variable before asking about its health in your project environment.

For some, *consequences* has a negative connotation. In the context of the Performance System, a consequence can be positive (rewarding) or negative (punishing). Research has shown that rewarding good performance is a more effective and lower-maintenance consequence strategy than punishing all possible forms of substandard performance.

Consequences are not merely formal rewards (salary increases, promotions, time off, a company car) and punishments (dismissal, suspension, bad ratings on a performance appraisal). Most of these types of consequences cannot—and should not—be provided frequently. Day-to-day consequences with impact include thank-yous, public recognition, and prestigious or challenging assignments.

Executives need to customize the consequences for individuals and teams. A consequence that is positive to Elizabeth may be negative to Robert. Examples of consequences that are perceived as positive to some and negative to others are international travel, being asked to present project results to executives, greater independence, and supervisory responsibility.

Consequences don't come solely from management. Derek's customers, peers, and subordinates may be as or more powerful sources of consequences than his boss.

Consequences don't have to be administered externally. Many of the most powerful consequences come from the work itself. Some initiative work is fun. Some is stimulating. Some is a welcome change from normal tasks. Some isn't pleasant, but is going to make life on the job easier or better. Some increases pride and job security by improving the health and performance of the organization.

Caution: Do not assume that the work is intrinsically rewarding. From your executive perspective, it may seem that it should be; however, the individual(s) involved may not see it that way. Perception is reality.

Many executives are uncomfortable dealing with consequences because they see them as a function of individuals' psychological makeup, an arena that they don't feel is their domain or that they don't think they are qualified to probe and analyze. The good news: you won't need a couch, a 50-minute timer, or practice asking, "How do you feel about that?" People welcome the opportunity to tell you what they find rewarding and punishing (as long as they're not punished for telling you what they find punishing).

Consequences are the 900-pound gorilla of culture. Performers in a rewarding environment will often flourish in spite of weaknesses in other components of their Performance System.

To assess the consequences in your project culture, consider these questions:

- Do people refrain from recommending an improvement because they justifiably assume that they will be expected to lead the improvement project?

- Is being assigned to a project seen as a vote of confidence in a person's ability or as an indication that he or she can be spared from ongoing work?

- Do people who are assigned to projects see themselves as having been given an opportunity to have a greater impact or as having been removed from the action?

- Do people who are assigned to projects perceive project assignments as punishing because they represent additional work heaped on an already full plate?

- Are project managers and team members recognized solely for their day-job contributions and not for their project work?

- Are projects perceived as environments that are rife with learning and networking opportunities or as cesspools of frustration, pressure, and grunt work?

- Do people who achieve project objectives on time and on budget get ahead in the organization?

- In long-term projects, are there rewards for accomplishing interim milestones?

- Are consequences consistent? (For example, are project teams being rewarded this month for meeting schedules regardless of cost, when last month they were punished for cost overruns that enabled them to meet the milestones?)

At the appliance manufacturer, consequences did not initially support initiatives. People who made above-and-beyond project contributions got little recognition. On the other hand, those who allowed even minor missteps in ongoing operations were drawn and quartered.

Project managers and team members perceived—and in this arena, perception is reality—that it was punishing to dedicate time to project work. For example, one line manager gave an individual who was serving as project manager for a cross-functional initiative an "unsatisfactory" rating in his annual performance review. The documented rationale was "insufficient attention to departmental priorities." Another project manager was able to keep up with her milestones only by increasing her average workweek by 10 hours. While the executives admired her dedication, they realized that it would take a long-term toll on her. Nor was that level of effort something that they could or should expect from others.

To get the company's strategic initiative program back on track, the executives had to move quickly. They considered adding a "project-goal accomplishment" section to performance appraisals. However, they felt that reformulating objectives for the 150 people directly involved in the 31 change projects would be an administrative nightmare. Furthermore, we helped them understand that providing frequent, meaningful rewards drives behavior change more than modifying a form that is completed once a year.

Marketing had recently designed and rolled out a successful customer loyalty program. Since that program lit a fire under the same people who were being asked to contribute to initiatives, the executives decided to use it as a model for their effort to align consequences with project excellence.

We helped the executives develop a campaign that they called the Project Rewards Program (PRP). The heart of the PRP is measuring performance against the project definitions, milestones, budgets, and roles specified in project plans. After each biweekly project meeting, sponsors award points to project managers based on project performance overall and on their personal contributions to that performance. Project managers, in turn, award points to each team member based on his or her performance vis-à-vis documented project expectations.

The Project Office (see Chapter 4) records individual point totals and each month gives the CEO a list of the top 10 project performers. The CEO publishes what has become known as his monthly "Project WOW" (Walk on Water) list. The Project WOW list has three purposes: it provides high-level recognition to those who are pushing their projects hard and getting results; it helps initiative contributors know how they are doing; and it demonstrates the CEO's support for those involved with projects, making it harder for others in the organization to obstruct project progress.

While the Project WOW list has motivational value, it is not tangible enough to change the company's initiative culture. To close this gap, the PRP includes a provision for individuals to accumulate their points and use them to "buy" rewards that are meaningful to them. For example, a certain number of points can be exchanged for a day off, additional discounts when purchasing the company's products, or tickets to sporting events.

The PRP has fueled an increase in initiatives achieving their objectives on time and on budget. It focuses people on their individual project responsibilities. It raises the profile of strategy implementation. And people find it to be fun.

This type of program may not address your initiative shortcomings. Or it may not fit your organization's culture. We've worked in organizations in which these types of incentives are perceived as demeaning or too cute. Other organizations don't thrive on internal competition. Installing a PRP-type program is just an option; aligning consequences with initiative expectations is not.

If a consequence effort centered on tangible rewards sounds as if it would fit your organization's culture, we would like to point out two land mines. First, tax law can classify these rewards as taxable "benefits in kind," taking the bloom off the reward rose. Second, the pendulum can swing so far to the project side that you replace disincentives for project contributions with disincentives for working on ongoing operations. You end up trading your headache for an upset stomach. Consequence management involves striking the right balance between initiative and day-job rewards.

In the organization profiled at the end of this chapter, executives are continually pulling the initiative consequence lever.

FEEDBACK: DO YOUR INITIATIVE CONTRIBUTORS KNOW WHERE THEY STAND?

Another important dimension of your initiative culture is feedback, which is the formal and informal information that project contributors receive about their performance. Consider these questions:

- Do project managers and team members get formal (performance review/appraisal) and informal (day-to-day) information on their project contributions?

- Is the feedback that they receive
  - Coming from all stakeholders (e.g., the sponsor, the initiative's target population, and their line managers)?
  - Understandable?
  - Sufficiently frequent and immediate?
  - Specific enough to guide performance?
  - Balanced (not overly skewed toward strengths or weaknesses)?
  - Delivered in a constructive, supportive manner?

If project managers and team members do not receive feedback on their contributions to initiatives, they are being sent a clear message: Projects are not an important part of your job. If they get project performance feedback, but it is inaccurate, too general to be helpful, only negative, or too delayed, their performance is likely to suffer. Even people with exemplary skills and self-confidence need to know where they stand.

The Project Rewards Program (PRP) in our appliance company is as focused on feedback as on consequences. Like all good feedback systems, the PRP's foundation is a set of expectations that includes both outputs and metrics. Fortunately, performance measurement was an accepted part of this company's culture; it merely needed to migrate that discipline from daily operations to the initiative environment.

The heart of the PRP—and the foundation for the incentive system described earlier—is the biweekly measurement of project managers' and team members' performance against the project objectives, milestones, budgets, and roles specified in the project plans.

Even if the PRP didn't contain formal consequences, initiative contributors would be reaping significant dividends from the clear expectations and the frequent, pinpointed, constructive feedback on their performance against those expectations.

PERFORMERS: DO YOU HAVE THE RIGHT PLAYERS ON THE INITIATIVE FIELD?

Once you have examined the work environment, it is time to determine if the right people are involved in your projects. The overarching question is, in a supportive environment, will the individuals who are currently assigned be able to make the needed contribution? For each project performer—and, here, think not only individuals, but also teams and groups, which are often less or more than the sum of the individuals who constitute them—consider:

> Do they have the mental and emotional capability to play their project role?

For example, do sponsors have the "leadership gene"? Do project managers have patience and attention to detail? Are team members capable of functioning in a group setting?

If the answer to any of these questions is no, you may have the wrong people involved or playing the wrong roles.

> Do they have the skills and knowledge to play their project role?

For example, do sponsors know how to guide a project without usurping the role of the project manager? Do they know how to energize a skeptical target population? Do project managers know how to develop a plan that includes the right information and the right level of detail? Do they know how to manage a team whose members may not formally report to them? Do team members have the technical proficiency necessary to carry out their assignments?

If the answer to any of these questions is no, you may need to supply training or coaching.

To ensure that the right people are put on the project field and to identify their training needs, we have helped some organizations construct Project Competency Models. These models describe the skills, knowledge, and experience required for exemplary performance in each project role described in Chapter 6. An example of a Project Competency Model appears in Figure 5-4.

FIGURE 5-4   A Project Manager Project Competency Model

Project Competency Area	Skills/Knowledge
Technical	Project management process, passport, and tool usage
	Project plan development in Microsoft Project
	Strategic and financial business-case development
	Business-process management
	Risk assessment and tracking
	Project issue resolution
People/ Performance	Project status communication (up, down, and sideways)
	Resource negotiation
	Performance expectation development and communication
	Performance environment development/improvement
	Feedback communication
	Conflict resolution
Project Content Specific	Lean manufacturing
	Inventory management
	Pharmaceutical compliance
	Managing in an environment of ambiguity and fast-changing priorities

Our appliance manufacturer is blessed with first-class talent. The value congruence, skills, industry experience, and work ethic of initiative contributors provide the raw material for strategy implementation success. However, analysis identified one gap in the performer component of the Performance System: project management skills. The vice president of human resources assumed responsibility for installing training and apprenticeship programs that provided current and future project managers with the skills they needed to carry out their initiative responsibilities.

OTHER DIMENSIONS OF THE CULTURAL LANDSCAPE

There are pervasive elements of culture that are not included in the examples just cited, but that have a significant influence on initiative success. They include the following:

- The degree of trust among superiors, subordinates, and peers
- The role played by organizational politics
- The level(s) at which decisions are made
- The basis for decisions (fact versus gut)
- The tolerance for risk
- The way meetings are run
- The nature of communication (frequency, tone, specificity, and vehicles)
- The pace of activities
- The attention span of executives

Each of these influences can be analyzed independently. However, we treat them within the framework of the Performance System. For example, decision levels influence the expectations in the situation. Communication is part of the situation and also part of feedback. Politics and risk play into consequences. We have found that viewing all cultural variables through the lens of the Performance System organizes, simplifies, and focuses the diagnosis and treatment of this complex dimension of strategy implementation.

ESTABLISHING A SUPPORTIVE
PROJECT CULTURE: A CASE STUDY

While an incentive program like our appliance company's Project Rewards Program can be useful in establishing and maintaining the momentum of strategy implementation, it cannot by itself create a culture that supports project delivery on a day-to-day basis. To achieve this objective, Performance-System thinking needs to be woven into the entire environment within which an organization "gets stuff done."

Reading Tom Peters's book *The Project 50*[1] caused the president of a pharmaceutical company's operations division to enlist our support in building an organization that would consistently deliver winning projects. Having designed and introduced the necessary structures, processes, and roles, we had to make it all stick by turning our attention to the design of the project culture.

Using the Performance System as our guide, we started by looking at how we could ensure that project performers had the skills and knowledge necessary to perform their project roles effectively.

To gain consensus on and codify the skills and knowledge needed, we built a Project Competency Model for sponsors, one for project managers, and one for team members. The competency categories were

- Technical project competencies (tools, templates, and processes)

- People and performance competencies (managing the human element)

- Competencies that were specific to a certain type of project (e.g., a product development project or a marketing project)

The model that we created for the company's project managers appears in Figure 5-4.

We constructed an initial Competency Profile for all those associated with initiative work. With input from other initiative contributors, individuals and their managers rate each person's proficiency at his or her project role as "expert," "competent," or "learning." We developed an assessment process for use on an ongoing basis.

The executive team then created a process for individual growth. Development Plans focus on a number of performance dimensions, including the skills and knowledge that individuals need to have in order to move to the expert level in their current role and the skills and knowledge that they need if they are to take on a more significant role—for example, to move from team member to project manager.

Using the Development Plans as guides, management builds individual competencies through training and coaching. The training curriculum includes courses covering various levels of Project Management Body of Knowledge[2]–based technical development, a "soft skills" course entitled "Managing People in Projects," and a sponsorship course that we imaginatively called "Project Sponsorship."

The coaching process begins with individuals and their coaches reviewing or creating their Development Plans. A project manager (PM) may be coached by a sponsor or by a more seasoned PM. A team member is typically coached by a PM. As projects progress, coaches not only mentor team members, but also update their Competency Profiles. As described later in this chapter, the development of project competencies has become a key component of an individual's performance appraisal.

Having ensured that the performers were holding up their portion of the Performance System, we assessed the degree to which the situation was aligned to support initiatives. The deployment of project role definitions, project management processes, and Project Competency Models established clear expectations. However, those actions didn't address all needs in the situation. People needed access to the right information and a physical environment that supported project work.

Experience has taught us that the best and easiest way to give project contributors access to the information they need is to provide them with a single software program on their desktop computer. The operations division's top team, with substantial input from the IT director, developed these software design specifications:

- Provide instant visibility for the current status of the overall portfolio.

- Display a "dashboard" that shows the current status of all individual projects.

- Enable senior management to drill down to whatever level of detail they require.

- Make "teachable moment" performance support, guidelines, and advice available to sponsors, PMs, and teams.

- Enable best-practices sharing among current and past project contributors.

- Support teams that have members in remote locations.

The company's IT wizards developed a "one-stop project shop." This intranet solution, anchored by Microsoft Project Central, allowed individuals to manage and share project plans and documentation online; access all project protocol and knowledge resources; review project, program, and portfolio status; assign and accept or decline work packages; submit status reports; and register for project management training courses.

The remaining weakness of the situation concerned the physical environment. The open space in which the majority of people sat was not conducive to initiative-team efficacy. The scarcity of meeting rooms compounded the problem. The teams found that they were continually distracted at their workstations. Impromptu project meetings were frequently held in the cafeteria.

The remedy lay in allocating specific space for initiative work. This area, dubbed "Project Land," consists of desks specifically reserved for those who want to pursue project work away from the distractions of their day-job environment. Meeting rooms are reserved for projects. The hub of Project Land is the Project Office, which is responsible for supporting and controlling all project activity, as outlined in Chapter 4.

While physical space may appear to be a minor matter, contributors found it extremely helpful to be able to go to a dedicated location to focus on project work. As one team member commented, it was "liberating and productive."

The final elements of the Performance System that we addressed were the high-impact areas of feedback and consequences. The CEO recognized outstanding project achievement with an incentive system similar to the Project Rewards Program described earlier. However, the real challenge was to embed project success into the ongoing feedback and reward system without compromising ongoing operations.

This organization, like many others, had experienced little success in its attempts to align project goals with annual objectives. Why? Because, unlike most of the measures that it used to judge people's performance, such as sales volume and production rate, project metrics did not feed comfortably into a yearly performance review. Initiatives generally weren't easily annualized. Many covered a period shorter than a year; some were longer. Some project managers needed to modify their objectives (one manager called this "refueling in flight") to align initiatives with changes in the external environment and/or internal priorities. As a result, project performance was not reflected on performance appraisals. Therefore, a significant component of people's energy was dedicated to activities that had no influence on their feedback, raises, bonuses, or promotion potential.

We introduced an objective-setting and appraisal process that meets the needs of a fast-changing project environment without either overwhelming or taking a back seat to operational goals. At the macro level, the system does not include specific project goals. Individual project performance ratings are the sum of performance reviews conducted by PMs and sponsors at appropriate project milestones.

The process follows these steps:

1. During the initiative definition phase, a PM conducts an objective-setting meeting with each team member. During this meeting, the PM and the team member agree on

project-specific contributions and on the Development Plan, which is based on the Competency Profile described earlier.

2. At appropriate intervals throughout the project and formally as part of the project closeout, PMs appraise both dimensions of individual performance. The output of this appraisal is represented by a percentage score, which is forwarded to individuals' line managers for inclusion in their overall appraisal.

3. When developing an individual's objectives for the year, managers and employees reach consensus on the proportion of the rating that should be based on day-job performance and the proportion that should be based on project contributions.

4. During the year-end performance review, functional managers assess individuals against their day-job targets, to which they usually have firsthand exposure, and their consolidated initiative performance based on PM and/or sponsor reviews.

This feedback/consequences system accomplishes these objectives:

•   Individual appraisals are customized to the individuals' unique roles.

•   Individuals are not inappropriately rewarded or punished for spending time on day-job or project activities.

•   Individuals are not penalized for working on a project that, for legitimate reasons beyond their control, changes direction or thrust in midstream.

•   Assessments are done by those who are closest to individuals' performance.

•   Executives can determine the investment they are making in projects and—down to the individual level—the return on that investment. This accomplishment is significant in an organization in which the average employee devotes 50 percent of his or her time to project work.

FIGURE 5-5   Two Contrasting Cultures in Which Strategies
Must Be Implemented

Company A: Midsized Regional Bank	Company B: Large, Global Consumer Products Company
Process-oriented	Process-averse
Risk-averse	Comfortable taking big risks
Team-oriented	Built around individual "cowboys" at all levels
Hierarchical	Fervently antihierarchical
Analytical	From the hip
Uncomfortable with internal competition	Thrives on internal competition

YOUR UNIQUE CULTURE

While the Performance System is a generic tool, its application to your setting is unique. Your Initiative Culture has to be aligned with your overall culture. We have done strategy implementation work with two clients whose cultures couldn't be more different. Figure 5-5 highlights some of the differences.

Both organizations had strategies that needed to be implemented. Both recognized initiatives as the vehicles for that implementation. However, the project support environment in areas such as expectation setting and incentives had to be aligned with their cultures, which were not going to change anytime soon and which were, in both cases, a source of pride.

For example, let's examine the consequences dimension of the Performance System that was installed to support initiatives in each culture. Company A provides incentives for both results and exemplary use of the project management process. In Company B, the incentives are purely for results. In Company A, team successes are publicized and rewarded. In Company B, individuals are singled out for kudos. In Company A, interactions with senior management are a valued form of recognition. In Company B, strong initiative contributors are rewarded with trips and gift certificates.

COMMENT

When it comes to implementing strategic initiatives, selecting the right projects and a manageable project workload is not enough. Rigorous project definition and planning is not enough. Ensuring that each initiative has the right sponsor, project manager, and team members is not enough. The success of projects is heavily dependent on the support that is or is not provided by the culture, as reflected in the situations, performers, consequences, and feedback that make up the Performance System.

NOTES

1.   Tom Peters, *The Project 50* (New York: Alfred A Knopf, 1999).

2.   Project Management Institute Publications, *A Guide to the Project Management Body of Knowledge*, 2000 Edition, 2001.

ENGAGING
PROJECT TEAMS

*S*TRENGTH & TONE *(S&T) manufactures a wide range of exercise equipment that it sells to the home market. The top team has recently come down from the mountain with a new strategy. There are opportunities to expand S&T's share of the home market, particularly through new sales channels; however, the executives concluded that the most promising way to meet their ambitious growth targets is by pursuing, for the first time, the institutional market, which includes fitness centers, schools, hotels, prisons, and professional sports teams. This strategy has spawned a variety of market research and competitive analysis initiatives, the success of which will determine whether the strategy is viable and, if so, whether it can be successfully implemented.*

S&T has produced solid financial results. It is second to none in operational efficiency and effectiveness. However, it is far from exemplary in its project performance. Initiatives of all types—marketing, product development and commercialization, process improvement, structure change, system installation—are launched with great fanfare and executive support, but all too frequently they fail to achieve their objectives on time and on budget.

Unlike those in many other organizations, S&T's projects are not sacrificed on the altar of changing priorities or short attention spans. They are not abandoned because they don't make sense or are insufficiently funded. S&T's executives have concluded that the reason for project failure lies somewhere in the human dimension. The people who staff projects don't understand what is expected of them, are playing the wrong roles, are not well suited for their responsibilities, and/or are insufficiently skilled.

If S&T can't get its initiative performance to the level of its operational performance, its growth strategy will remain a dream, causing the company to languish among its industry's other small niche players who are struggling with single-digit growth.

FIGURE 6-1   Initiative Roles: A Critical Success Factor for Strategy Implementation

What's the most significant challenge facing senior executives who are intent on ensuring that initiatives are flawlessly executed? The president of one of our defense-industry clients said it best: "Getting the right resources assigned and freed up. People have day-to-day jobs. They have to be focused and aligned with the initiative. The workload is continually shifting. Initiatives need the best people, and they are already fully employed. Priorities need to be reestablished."

Let's assume that you have put in place the process we've outlined. You have your "initiative wish list" in hand (Chapter 2). You've winnowed that list and established priorities for the projects that remain (Chapter 3). Your structure (Chapter 4) and culture (Chapter 5) now support initiative deployment. Throughout the discussion of each of those success factors, we have made brief references to the roles that should be played in moving implementation from a portfolio of initiatives to a "job well done." Now that the initiative infrastructure has been established, it is appropriate to discuss those roles more fully (see Figure 6-1). Think of project teams as sports organizations, and the various contributors to project success as playing roles analogous to those played by the members of those organizations. We will begin with the roles you are most likely to play.

THE PROGRAM DIRECTOR: THE TEAM OWNER

Large change efforts often involve a portfolio of independent initiatives. To ensure integration and simplify reporting, executives frequently group "birds of a feather" projects together in a program. While the definition, objectives, contributors, and timeline of each project are unique, they contribute to the same overarching goal. For example, you may have a number of initiatives that would benefit from being grouped together in an outsourcing program. Others may find a natural home in a branding/positioning/marketing program. To ensure that the various projects mesh, we recommend designating an executive as the program director.

For example, the executive team of Strength & Tone, the company described at the beginning of this chapter, has formulated and validated its new strategy and is now ready to implement that strategy. The executive vice president of business development is serving as the program director. In this role, she oversees the overall Strategic Master Project Plan. That plan contains an initiative focused on exiting from the low-margin home barbell and exercise-video product lines, another on entering the school market, and a third on acquiring a company that will bring market intelligence and engineering talent to S&T. Each of these projects has its own sponsor, project manager, and team. The program director is, in effect, the strategy-implementation officer who makes sure that all of the projects related to the successful implementation of the business strategy have been defined and integrated into a focused plan of attack.

We asked one of our strategy clients, the president of a retail chain, for his biggest initiative execution challenge. He said, "It is not enough to have skilled project managers. I've found I need a single person to corral all strategic projects. I gave that responsibility to my chief administrative officer. It takes him away from some of his day-to-day duties, but it's worth it."

THE PROJECT SPONSOR: THE TEAM'S GENERAL MANAGER

As an executive, the role that you are most likely to play is that of project sponsor. For those initiatives with significant organizational impact, the sponsor is typically drawn from the ranks of the executive team. Where a project has a more modest effect, a lower-level manager is selected. In either case, a project sponsor is someone with "skin in the game," someone who is passionate about the success of the project and is willing to back up that passion with accountability. If an initiative is "owned" by an organizational entity, such as a business unit, product line, department, or country, the sponsor is usually the person who is responsible for that part of the business.

If an initiative is cross-functional, the sponsor is usually the executive with the most zeal and the most at stake. A sponsor

- Forges and articulates the initiative *vision*. The vision is the overarching project goal. It is an achievable aspiration. It connects the project, no matter how humble, to the strategy of the business. For example
  - "Establish a best-in-class customer-service department."
  - "Reduce product development time to six months."
  - "Become the number two player in the Greater China market."
  This vision often serves as the centerpiece of the Project Statement discussed in Appendix A.

- Provides the *leadership* for the project. As with leadership in other areas of the business, this role includes mobilizing, energizing, providing context and connections to other initiatives, coaching, communicating, and motivating.

- Ensures that the right quality and quantity of *resources* are dedicated to the project. The up-front dimension of this role involves freeing up the people and the money required for project success. The ongoing role is to resolve resource issues in response to shifting priorities, the evolving needs of the project, and others' demands for the project's people and funds.

- Removes nonresource project *obstacles*, such as policy constraints, lack of support from key stakeholders, and conflicts with other initiatives or ongoing operations.

- Provides *rewards* for project performance. Rewards are often not tangible; they may include thank-yous, public recognition, visibility at senior levels, autonomy, or challenging assignments. In addition to accentuating the positive, the sponsor needs to eliminate the negative. Project managers and team members should not be punished (e.g., by their day-job manager or peers) for dedicating

their time and talent to the success of a project. Rewards
are a key dimension of the initiative excellence culture
that is discussed in Chapter 5.

- Serves as project *spokesperson and conscience* on the executive team. The sponsor ensures that the project gets the
executive agenda time and mind share that it deserves.
One aspect of this role is arranging periodic executive
briefings by the project manager, as we outline in subsequent paragraphs here and in Chapter 8.

Like any effective sports team general manager, the sponsor avoids taking on the tactical "field leader" role, which
should be played by the project manager, profiled later. The
only exceptions are bet-the-company or close-to-the-vest
strategic initiatives, in which the sponsor may also be the project manager.

Here are some examples of the behaviors exhibited by
exemplary sponsors with whom we've had the pleasure of
working:

- A frequent sponsor of marketing initiatives in a beverage
company had an atypical but effective policy: She would
personally take responsibility for one "work package"
(component of an overall project plan). While some executives wouldn't be comfortable getting into the trenches,
she found that it enabled her to stay close to the real
world of initiative execution. And it gained her loyalty
and credibility that caused others to go the extra mile in
making project contributions.

- An employee attitude survey in a European bank
showed that minorities did not think that they were
given the same opportunities as others. This spawned a
high-profile/high-sensitivity diversity project. The draft
project plan included an array of actions that ranged
from adding a diversity review step to the corporate
communications process to retooling the succession-
planning system. In spite of pressure to move quickly,
the sponsor was not comfortable championing these
steps until he was sure that they addressed the root cause

of the problem. He commissioned an analysis that showed both that the dissatisfied employees were clustered in one division and that the proposed actions, while noble in intent, would not have addressed the cause of the discontent. The initiative was redesigned to focus on the division with the problem and on the cause, which was the lack of transparency in the compensation and promotion processes.

- Little things can make a big difference. A CEO who personally sponsored a strategic initiative asked that a review meeting be attended not only by the project manager, but also by the other team members. Before the meeting, he scheduled a briefing that included the names of the team members and one or two facts about each. This information enabled him to address the team members personally during the social time he arranged before the start of the meeting.

When asked for his biggest strategy-implementation challenge, the defense contractor president cited at the beginning of this chapter said, without hesitation,

> Most people at all levels don't want to do anything differently. They resist change. Strategy requires doing things differently. I need to find a champion or two to make it happen. All I need is a couple of people out there selling. Strategy implementation is a sales job; we can only force/intimidate people so much.

The best platform for these champions is the sponsor role. The sponsor may also form and chair a steering team, the roles of which are described in the next section.

THE STEERING TEAM AND/OR PORTFOLIO MANAGEMENT COMMITTEE: THE TEAM'S BOARD OF DIRECTORS

A major cross-functional or cross-division change initiative, such as integrating an acquisition or improving a companywide order-fulfillment process, benefits from having a steering team, which some organizations call a program board or project board. Chaired by the sponsor, steering teams typically include the project manager and the head of each key stakeholder group. Their purpose is to

- Help the sponsor establish the project vision and direction.

- Build commitment to the change.

- Monitor the progress of the project and redirect it if necessary.

- Approve a project's passage from one phase to the next.

- Ensure that the project has the priority and resources it deserves.

- Oversee project communication.

- Eliminate cross-organization conflicts that could compromise project success.

- Ensure project closeout, including lessons learned.

At the corporate or business unit level, the CEO or his or her equivalent may chair a portfolio management committee composed of the program directors, sponsors, and other members of the executive team. This team plays the same roles as the steering team, but across a set of programs or projects. While the steering team serves as an initiative's board of directors, the portfolio management committee is the board for the entire project waterfront. It ensures that the entire portfolio is strategically aligned, integrated, and communicated.

THE PROJECT MANAGER: THE TEAM'S COACH

The project manager plays the role of the coach in basketball or American football and the manager in baseball or soccer. Every project, small or large, short-term or long-term, should have a project manager (PM) who develops the game plan and guides the team to victory. The roles of the PM are

- Planner/scheduler
- Resource estimator/coordinator
- Logistics manager
- Risk manager
- Monitor
- Facilitator
- Cheerleader
- Change manager
- People/performance manager
- Methods/tools (automated and manual) provider
- Documenter
- Updater
- Communicator (up, down, and sideways)
- Information clearinghouse

While this is rarely in the formal responsibility description, most PMs also play these roles:

- Conscience
- Nag
- Father/mother confessor
- Materials schlepper
- Software troubleshooter
- Scapegoat
- Executive surrogate

The extent of executive support, the capability of team members, and the adequacy of funding are critical factors in project success; however, strengths in these areas cannot compensate for a weak PM. On the other hand, a strong PM can see that leadership and resource gaps are filled.

PM selection criteria include

- Experience in managing projects
- Mastery of the project management process and tools (see Chapter 7 and Appendix A)
- Ability to dedicate the time necessary for project success
- Attention to detail
- Obsession with achieving objectives on time and on budget
- Ability to communicate, orally and in writing
- Skills and experience managing/influencing people, including those who are not direct reports
- Ability to juggle multiple responsibilities
- Flexibility
- Tenacity
- Patience

PMs may or may not have what we call "content," which is experience or expertise in specific project activities. They may or may not be affected by the change; however, too much stake in the outcome could compromise their objectivity.

In a major project, the PM may oversee subproject managers, who play the roles listed earlier for a component of the overall project. Sub-PMs are the equivalent of offensive and defensive coordinators in American football or passing and kicking coaches in rugby.

A set of projects that are all part of the same program, such as entering a new market or installing an enterprisewide information system, may require a program director who serves as the über-project manager, coordinating the interfaces among the individual projects within that initiative. That role has been described previously.

You may want to encourage or require full-time project managers and those who are assigned particularly high-impact projects to complete the rigorous process of being certified by the Project Management Institute as Project Management Professionals.[1] You should not be surprised that there is a project manager certification program. As the volume of initiative activity has increased, project management has evolved from a role to a profession; 4.5 million people in the United States—3.3 percent of employed individuals—regard project management as their vocation. The profession's size in the rest of the world totals more than 12 million people. A complex and growing library of expertise and tools is being codified in the Project Management Body of Knowledge.[2]

THE PROJECT TEAM: THE PLAYERS

A project team may have as few as three part-time members. A massive project with a large number of subprojects (responding to a regulatory compliance warning and launching a major new product come to mind) may have dozens of project team members, many of whom are deployed full-time.

Each project team member—alone or as part of a group—produces or contributes to one or more of the project deliverables or "work packages." Tasks may be as diverse as lobbying Congress, writing code, hiring contractors, negotiating leases, and moving filing cabinets. Selection criteria for project team members include

- Technical proficiency in the area to which they are assigned

- Ability to dedicate the time necessary to do exemplary work

- Skill and experience in working as part of a team, often across organizational lines

- Ability to meet deadlines, often under significant pressure

- Flexibility

- Ability to juggle multiple responsibilities

If this description looks suspiciously like a description of the people that everyone wants for everything, you read it right.

It is not unusual to expand the project team to include individuals who don't bring any technical specialty to the table but whose commitment is critical to project success. Hands-on participation may generate broader and deeper support than that which is developed through a compelling sales pitch. Union stewards, opinion leaders, and first-line supervisors often fall into this category.

An effective project team contains not only appropriate functional representation and technical knowledge/skills, but also the right mix of personalities, styles, and intellectual orientations. For example, you may want a product development project team to include a never-compromise idealist, a highly creative thinker, a "that will never work" crepe hanger, a just-the-facts analyst, a synthesizer, a feet-on-the-ground implementer, and an administrator. Team performance can also be enhanced by a balance of personality types. Effective teams often use the Myers-Briggs Type Indicator[3] to ensure this diversity. In well-oiled project teams, each individual is expected to make a contribution, such as those limned by Meredith Belbin,[4] that matches team needs and individual strengths.

THE TARGET POPULATION: THE FANS

The target population, often called "stakeholders," is made up of those on whom the initiative will have an impact. They are not merely fans with a bias toward a project "win" for the home team, but ones with a sizable wager riding on the outcome. For example,

- In a restructuring initiative, the target population is the people whose reporting relationships will be changed.

- In a business process improvement initiative, the target population is the people who will work in, provide input to, and receive the output of the new process.

- In a computer-system installation initiative, the target population is made up of those who use the system and its outputs.

- In a relocation initiative, the target population is made up of those who will move and those who interact with them.

Even though the project team members represent the target population, the entire stakeholder group requires information about the project. Without regular communication to the target population, productivity will suffer, the rumor mill will produce conclusions that are not based in reality, and key people will become unnecessarily paranoid.

Project success may also require the target population to provide inputs to the project team. Those inputs include information, analysis, technical advice, implementation obstacles, and personal concerns.

THE PROJECT MANAGEMENT FACILITATORS: THE ADVISORS

Regardless of the project experience of the sponsor, the project manager, the project team, and the program director, most projects need to be guided by experts in the project management process described in Appendix A. These individuals serve in the same capacity as black belts in a Six Sigma program. At the macro level, they provide methods and tools and troubleshoot projects that have gone off the rails. At the micro level, they plan and guide project meetings, challenging and stretching team thinking, serving as the conscience of project management best practices, ensuring that everyone participates, managing the pace, and documenting outputs in the chosen software program (see the discussion later in the chapter). They are an organization's experts in how the project game should be played.

A facilitator does not provide answers to the technical questions that are bound to surface during a project—For example, "Can this activity be automated cost-effectively?" or "What's the best way to install lean manufacturing?" He or she guides the discussion, ensuring that the people in all of the roles we outlined are successfully answering the right questions as they solve problems and make decisions. In that sense, a facilitator is more like the Sherpa who guides others up the project mountain than like the person in the saffron robe who sits at the top of the mountain dispensing wisdom. In organizations with a Project Office, described in Chapter 4, facilitators reside in or are coordinated by that department.

SOFTWARE: A DIFFERENT KIND OF TEAM MEMBER

There's another role in projects, but it's a "what" rather than a "who": project management software. The good news: Software can make significant contributions to initiative deployment. The bad news: It can't do it all. A project sponsor or project manager can't turn management over to a software program any more than sports team coaches can expect robust databases and automated expert systems to tell them what to do in every game situation. Project management software *can*

- Document, format, and display the relationships among project steps
- Highlight the critical path of project steps
- Display the resources that are necessary at each stage of a project
- Display project plans and status in a user-friendly fashion
- Speed communication via LCD projections, hard copies, or e-mail attachments
- Draw attention to project overruns and bottlenecks
- Facilitate modifying the project plan and updating the status as new information or circumstances arise and the project progresses

   Project management software *cannot*

- Tell you if project steps are missing, poorly defined, or illogically sequenced
- Assess the quality with which an activity is being performed

- Make decisions regarding resource deployment, priorities, or interfaces
- Manage the human element of project success
- Resolve project issues

Project management software provides the same benefits and shortcomings as other software applications. Just as word processing software doesn't write proposals for you and spreadsheet software doesn't make your cash flow decisions, project management software does not manage projects. It is a valuable tool, but it is not a substitute for human judgment.

PROJECT ROLES: A CASE STUDY

We worked with a mid-sized pharmaceutical company that had a history of implementing change initiatives slowly, expensively, and with a dysfunctional level of political infighting. For an initiative to be successful, it had to surmount process and structure barriers. Each project was an island that didn't connect to a master plan or to other projects, employed its own methodology, and had a unique status-reporting format.

This situation got the attention of the executive team, and with good reason: The Food and Drug Administration had just threatened to close a plant for noncompliance, which spawned a number of projects. In addition, the company either had just launched or was about to launch several "bet-the-company" projects related to areas of new drug development and commercialization, capacity expansion, and computer-system installation. Its project portfolio contained 31 projects that needed to be guided and monitored at the executive level.

Two persistent weaknesses that compromised this company's strategy implementation were role definition and execution. For example, individuals were designated as project managers, but the role had never been clearly defined. As a result, inappropriate people were selected. Furthermore, PMs had no clear charter of authority, especially in the areas of directing people and marshaling resources. They weren't seeking more power, just an understanding of what they were expected to do.

Projects had sponsors, but these individuals were universally perceived as being too passive. They recognized that they were responsible for project outcomes, but they were unclear about their contribution to those outcomes. Some of them were all too willing to sign off on project requests without knowing what they were approving. Few of them looked above the hubbub of project activity, scanned the variables influencing project success, proactively identified obstacles, and took action to remove those obstacles.

To address their need for greater role clarity and definition, members of the Project Office defined these roles and trained people to play them properly:

- *A program director,* who reports to the CEO and is responsible for successfully delivering the entire portfolio of strategic initiatives. He or she is also the "owner" of the processes, systems, and capabilities needed to facilitate the delivery of those initiatives across the company.

- *Project sponsors,* who, because they are focused on strategic projects, are senior executives. They are accountable for delivering the benefits from the projects assigned to them. A large part of their role is guiding, supporting, and running interference for their project managers.

- *Project managers,* who are responsible for ensuring that projects are appropriately defined, thoroughly planned, and smoothly implemented. Their performance is measured against project performance (results), schedule, and budget goals.

- *Project team members,* who produce the project deliverables.

- *Project "black belts,"* who are the experts in the project management process outlined in Appendix A. Their role is to support complex projects by helping project managers plan, manage stakeholders, negotiate for resources, and resolve issues. In addition, they facilitate activities that keep, or get, a project on track.

The executive team also formed two formal decision-making groups that are responsible for exercising the right level of governance over projects, programs, and the portfolio as a whole. These are

- *Project and program boards* for each major project and program, or family of related projects. Such boards review and approve plans for each stage of a project and sanction a project's move from one stage to the next. They also provide project managers with the support they need to deliver projects, to ensure that projects are properly closed, and to ensure that project results are correctly evaluated and communicated. Each board includes the project sponsor, the project manager (typically a senior representative of the function most affected by the change), and often a representative of the target population.

- *A portfolio management committee,* whose role is to ensure that all projects within the portfolio maintain their alignment with strategic and operational goals, have the quality and quantity of resources to deliver the agreed-upon results, are effectively sponsored and managed, and have appropriate levels and methods of communication. This committee, chaired by the CEO, is made up of the program director and a number of the key project sponsors. It is the conscience and guardian of strategy implementation.

While the volume and importance of the strategic initiatives in this company more than justified this infrastructure of roles, it may be overly bureaucratic for your requirements. The key need in all organizations—regardless of the amount or complexity of initiative activity—is for each of these roles to be played. If initiatives can get the support and contributions they need from people wearing multiple hats and without new committees, great.

A WORD ON STRUCTURE

It is not sufficient to clearly define and appropriately assign these roles. People are helped or hindered by the organizational structure in which they function. In organizations that carry out nonproject work, the structure has a major influence on the interactions between project activities and ongoing operations. The need to build a project-supportive structure, possibly including a Project Office that coordinates all project effort, is so important that we devoted Chapter 4 to this topic.

YOUR ROLES

Regardless of the structure that you put in place, there are project success contributions that can be made only by you and your fellow executives. You will only occasionally be a project manager. You will rarely be a project team member. However, you play seven critical roles:

- *Project initiator.* Based on your unique and panoramic perspective on the organization's needs, you create strategic and operational projects.

- *Project priority setter.* You want to avoid the "too-much-on-the-plate" syndrome. Individually (for your area) and as a member of the top team (for the enterprise as a whole), you ensure that the organization isn't taking on more projects than it can handle and that the projects that are underway are implementing the strategy and addressing the most critical tactical business issues. (See Chapter 3.)

- *Program integrator.* When the scope, impact, and diversity of a change warrant a program director, that role must be filled by an executive.

- *Project champion.* This is the sponsor role that was described earlier.

- *Project resource provider.* You ensure that projects are appropriately staffed and funded.

- *Project support-system creator.* You install the organization structure (described in Chapter 4) and the culture (the expectations and reward systems described in Chapter 5) that promote project success.

- *Process patron.* While you don't have to immerse yourself
  in the steps in an initiative management process such as
  the one outlined in Appendix A, you need to be sure that
  a common language and approach are in place. That is
  the topic covered in Chapter 7.

COMMENT

Each role is a critical piece of the strategy implementation
game plan. A team with talented players and a weak coach—
i.e., project manager—rarely wins. Conversely, an exemplary
coach is limited by the talent of his or her players, or project
team members. If the general manager (the project sponsor)
lacks vision, provides minimal support, or interferes, the team
won't reach its potential. And, regardless of the win-loss
record, the fans (the target population) ultimately determine
whether the team succeeds or fails.

NOTES

1. See the certification process in the Professional Certifica-
    tions section of www.pmi.org.
2. Project Management Institute Publications, *A Guide to
    the Project Management Body of Knowledge: 2000 Edition,*
    2001.
3. Otto Kroeger and Janet Thuesen, *Type Talk: The Sixteen
    Personality Types That Influence How We Live, Love, and
    Work* (New York: Delacorte, 1988).
4. R. Meredith Belbin, *Team Roles at Work* (Oxford: Butter-
    worth Heinemann, 1993).

C H A P T E R

7

USING A COMMON PROCESS TO MANAGE INITIATIVES

*J*EANNE STRICKLAND IS FRUSTRATED. *The majority owner and president of Strickland Dairy, Jeanne realizes that her company has grown to the point where it can no longer be managed by a group of confidants whom she can gather around a table with a half-hour's notice. Most of the people who worked with Jeanne's father in the dairy's early days have retired, passing their mantles to a young, impatient, business-educated class of managers. Strickland now has farms, processing facilities, and distribution centers in a number of states. The product line has expanded beyond milk and cheese to include a wide range of dairy and soy products. Customer groups include not only grocery stores, but also fast-food outlets, health food stores, and in-company cafeterias.*

Jeanne is pleased with the extent and pace of change and growth. Her frustration comes from a side effect of that evolution: ineffective, inefficient communication. She and her team use e-mail and voicemail. They meet—face to face, via conference call, and occasionally even by videoconference—whenever a real-time dialogue is needed. However, their exchanges are rambling, circular, and inconclusive.

These lapses are particularly apparent in communication related to special projects. Strickland has standard templates for reporting on and troubleshooting day-to-day operations. However, project meetings sound like the United Nations without translators. At any given point in the discussions, one person is describing project intent, another is outlining actions, a third is bringing up risks, and yet another is focused on resources. This cross-communication makes project meetings inefficient and painful. Furthermore, Jeanne and her executive team—as well as people at lower levels—frequently leave initiative decision making and status meetings muttering, "Didn't we sit through the same meeting last month?" By any objective measure, Strickland Dairy would not get high marks for either the success or the efficiency of its projects. She doesn't understand why the company's project planning and deployment isn't as focused and effective as its business processes and troubleshooting.

THE NEED FOR A COMMON LANGUAGE

Jeanne Strickland needs a robust, user-friendly approach to Initiative Management. She needs consistency in the way people think about projects. Call it a methodology, a process, a protocol, a template, or a tool kit, Strickland needs a common language (see Figure 7-1).

Language is the organizing principle for thought, and it serves as the structure for discourse. If an organization approaches its greatest challenges—and no challenge is more formidable than implementing strategy—with a common language and approach, it increases its odds of success.

Is your organization populated with a variety of purchased or home-grown project management approaches, each of which has its own framework, lexicon, level of effectiveness, and ownership? If so, you are not alone. Deploying a single process across your organization—a *lingua franca* for

FIGURE 7-1   Initiative Management Process: A Critical Success Factor
for Strategy Implementation

strategy implementation—has many benefits, including the
following:

- Installing an Initiative Management discipline that ensures
  that all of the essential steps are covered in each project

- Enabling project managers and project team members
  across functions and regions to follow the same steps and
  use the same terms, improving efficiency and facilitating
  communication

- Simplifying and standardizing initiative reporting to
  executives and managers, who need to monitor progress
  and make directional decisions

SELECTING A COMMON PROCESS

Why reinvent the wheel? It would be natural to identify the function or species of project that has been most successful, such as manufacturing cost-reduction projects, product-development initiatives, or marketing campaign projects, and migrate its methodology across the company. While that may work, beware: if the approach was not designed with a general portfolio of projects in mind, it may hinder rather than help their execution. Many executives, flush with the success of an information technology system installation or product rollout, take a step backward when they attempt to migrate the approach used on the successful project to initiatives that aren't suited to its techniques and language.

For example, we once helped a financial institution identify and set priorities on a set of strategic initiatives. We then asked the director of change (his role and title are another story) how comfortable he was with his organization's implementation capability. "No problem," he responded. "We have a program office team, or POT, that takes the lead. They have lots of experience with projects."

A few weeks later, it became apparent that the change program was not progressing as intended. We were asked to unearth the reasons and recommend corrective actions. The more we learned about this company's approach to project deployment, the more it became clear that the POT acronym was apt.

The POT was originally set up to deliver IT projects, and the company's process was well engineered to meet that need. However, most people beyond Information Systems saw the process as a mysterious black box. Those who lifted the lid were confronted with mind-numbing templates, user-painful control documents, and arcane reporting techniques. There was no arguing with the success of the process in the IT world; however, it didn't fit other types of projects. As a result, those outside Information Systems adhered to the mandatory process only until their department secured funding. Thereafter, each project team developed and followed its own process.

Should there be a process that you can use on all species of projects? Our answer is yes, with this caveat: the commonality should be in steps, sequence, and tools. Project approval and control (the heart of the POT process) may need to be different in different environments.

While you will want to develop a set of methodology-selection criteria that fit your unique situation, here are some attributes to look for in a common process:

- It has a track record of successfully implementing strategic and tactical initiatives.

- It fits all types of initiatives (e.g., IT projects, marketing projects, product development projects, and organization structure projects).

- It meets the needs of all functions and geographies.

- It is robust enough to accommodate projects of all levels of complexity.

- It is user-friendly enough to be used by people who are not certified project managers or frequent project team members.

- It facilitates communication up, down, and sideways. A key aspect of this communication is providing executives with the type and level of detail that they need to guide initiatives.

- It fits the culture.

PROCESS DETAILS: WHAT DO YOU NEED TO KNOW?

As an executive, you will rarely find yourself in the project manager or project team member roles described in Chapter 6. As a result, you probably don't need or want to get tangled in the weeds of the technical aspects of the Initiative Management tool kit. After all, at your level you may have little need to be familiar with the alternative forms of work breakdown structure or the pros and cons of value engineering. However, you do need

- To be assured that your project managers are employing tested, structured, practical, common methods

- To understand enough about the process to respond intelligently when you are presented with a recommendation cast in its framework and employing its tools

- To take the lead in the up-front steps in the process, which establish project direction

Your need for detail is one dimension of your executive style. If you are comfortable knowing that we have developed an Initiative Management process that fulfills the criteria just mentioned, this chapter should be sufficient. If you want to examine the steps in that process and see a comprehensive example of its use, please see Appendix A.

Unlike people management, conflict resolution, and culture transformation, Initiative Management has an official repository of standards and practices, the Project Management Body of Knowledge, commonly referred to as *PMBOK*.[1] The process outlined in Appendix A conforms to this standard.

INTRODUCING A PROCESS TO DELIVER STRATEGIC INITIATIVES: A CASE STUDY

We worked with a consumer products company's top team as they identified and set priorities on their project portfolio. These executives were comfortable that this set of initiatives—which focused disproportionately on product development and marketing—would implement their newly formulated strategy. However, they were not at all comfortable with their ability to execute. The CEO said, "We don't have much in the way of a project management process around here. At best, I am kept up to date on project progress verbally. At worst, I am only reminded about a project when it needs additional funding. The only project plans I see are those presented by consultants."

The team concluded that initiative management discipline would remove a good deal of their skepticism regarding the organization's ability to implement its strategy. We were asked to help develop the appropriate process and templates.

We began by identifying the methods that were currently in use. We found that some individuals in the information systems department used a methodology called the Structured Systems Analysis and Design Method. Most new-product development projects employed another protocol, called PRINCE2, the results of which ranged from moderately successful to downright embarrassing. An example of the latter: In a recent new-product introduction, a high-priced market research study projecting the amount of cannibalization was completed two months after the new product had been launched! Effective Initiative Management would have either brought the research in on time or delayed the launch until its findings were analyzed. The significant cannibalization that the study predicted came about; had the executives known this, they would have reconfigured the product, delayed the launch, initiated incentives for buying the old product, or aborted the launch.

Outside of information systems and product development projects, we could find no consistency of Initiative Management roles, tools, or structure. All too often, project meetings were simply forums for information sharing and whining.

Armed with this understanding of the sorry state of the existing initiative execution environment, we began developing a process that would meet the company's needs. The first step was to establish boundaries and requirements. The top team agreed that the process would initially be deployed on strategy implementation projects, so that set of needs guided the team members' thinking as they established these criteria:

- Provide the vehicle for planning, organizing, administering, and controlling the delivery of all the projects needed to implement the strategy quickly and effectively.

- Provide all project contributors with clear performance expectations and specific steps to follow.

- Provide a common language to facilitate communication among all people affected by strategic change projects.

- Eliminate overlaps and gaps among projects.

- Facilitate working across department lines when required.

- Make strategy implementation top of mind by keeping plans and progress constantly visible.

- Enable speedy identification of assumptions that have proved false, triggering decisions regarding possible project delay, rescoping, or cancellation.

- Provide the foundation on which to build Initiative Management capability across the business.

To fulfill these requirements, the team and we developed the process summarized in Figure 7-2, which is a customized version of the framework presented in Appendix A.

The executives vowed not to revert to their "above-the-action" posture of the past. As a result, we thoroughly discussed, decided upon, and documented their role in each of the five phases.

Because the success of the company's strategy was heavily dependent upon new products, we developed a product-development process that was consistent with the generic process, but also incorporated specific steps and controls that were unique to that set of activities.

Having developed the Initiative Management "life cycle," the executives commissioned a small team to work with us to select the tools that would be used at each step. Included in the tool kit were

- Value management techniques in "Assess Idea"

- Critical path method in "Sequence Deliverables"

- Potential Problem Analysis in "Protect Plan"

- Earned value ratios in "Monitor Project"

The top team realized that even a robust, tailored Initiative Management process would not thrive in a hostile environment. To maximize support:

FIGURE 7-2   A Snapshot of One Company's Initiative Management Process

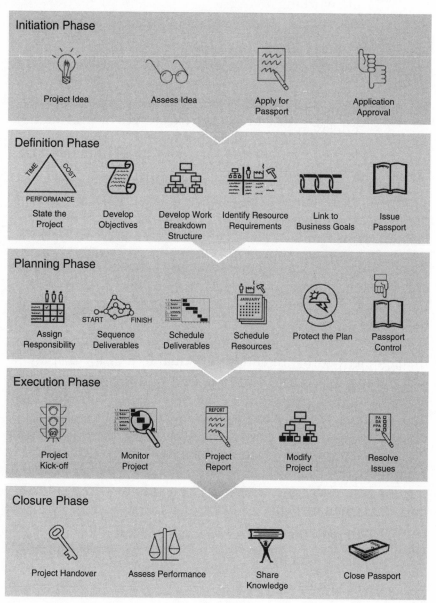

Initiation Phase

Project Idea   Assess Idea   Apply for Passport   Application Approval

Definition Phase

State the Project   Develop Objectives   Develop Work Breakdown Structure   Identify Resource Requirements   Link to Business Goals   Issue Passport

Planning Phase

Assign Responsibility   Sequence Deliverables   Schedule Deliverables   Schedule Resources   Protect the Plan   Passport Control

Execution Phase

Project Kick-off   Monitor Project   Project Report   Modify Project   Resolve Issues

Closure Phase

Project Handover   Assess Performance   Share Knowledge   Close Passport

- The high-powered program director was made the formal process owner and was measured on its performance.

- Everyone who contributed to project success was trained in the process. Those with a hands-on role were trained in the use of the tools.

- Project results and status measures were supplemented by process use measures. (The executives now cared not only where initiatives went, but how they got there.)

- The reward system was restructured to provide incentives for exemplary project contributions.

COMMENT

A solid Initiative Management process is no substitute for talent, passion, and hard work. However, talent, passion, and hard work that aren't channeled through a common process tend to go down blind alleys, confuse those who need to be on board, and waste resources. As discussed in Chapter 6, project management software can be a valuable tool for displaying and modifying the breakdown of work, the sequence of steps, and schedules. However, it is not a substitute for the judgment and interaction that need to occur during activities such as objective setting, plan protection, and project communication. Nor does it address the people challenges that we discussed in Chapter 5. Building commitment, resolving conflict, negotiating for resources, and providing rewards require leadership and management skills. Those skills separate stellar projects from those that drop out of the race or merely limp to the finish line.

NOTES

1.   Project Management Institute Publications, *A Guide to the Project Management Body of Knowledge: 2000 Edition*, 2001.

8

MONITORING
INITIATIVES

*E*VERY DAY, ANGELA BETTINCOURT UNDERSTANDS *more about
how her role as an executive differs from the other roles she has
played in various positions during her 20-year rise through
the ranks of VMB, Ltd., a full-service insurance company. As the
newly minted vice president of operations, she is the de facto chief
operating officer of a 1,500-person company with annual revenue of
€200 million. She understands that her focus needs to be on strategy
and leadership, not tactics and management.*

*However, she hasn't shed her penchant for detail and has no
desire to change that aspect of her style. While she has learned to
resist the urge to use her experience to tell subordinates how to do
their jobs, she is not comfortable making a decision without an in-
depth understanding of the situation. Furthermore, she is not willing to manage a business in which she is not close to day-to-day
activities.*

*Angela has systems in place for monitoring ongoing opera-
tions. In addition to staying on top of financial performance, she
receives and digests regular information on customer acquisition*

and retention, claim-processing time, claim volume, and employee satisfaction.

However, one aspect of the business is not included in her regular reports: special projects. Initiatives focused on business-process improvement, market research, and new-product development—all critical to implementing the VMB strategy—are major resource consumers; however, they are not formally on her radar screen. Angela believes that this mission-critical aspect of the business is out of her control. These initiatives have project managers who are usually able to respond to any of Angela's requests for information. However, she doesn't think that executive understanding of strategic-initiative status should rely solely on her inquiries. And, she's not sure she knows what questions to ask.

Unlike some of her colleagues, Angela is unwilling to manage by exception. She is not comfortable with their "If I don't hear anything, I'll assume that everything's OK" approach. Without imposing productivity-draining bureaucracy, she wonders how she can incorporate Initiative Reporting/Monitoring into her oversight of the performance of the business (see Figure 8-1).

If you've got the right people sponsoring and staffing an initiative and you have a sound project plan, you can focus your attention elsewhere, right? Sure, and a basketball coach can put talented players on the court with a good game plan and go fishing. No matter how clear your crystal ball, unforeseen external and internal changes will necessitate adjustments to most projects. We're reminded of an age-old military adage: "A battle plan survives only until the first encounter with the enemy." In this case, the potential "enemies" include

- Customers, competitors, suppliers, technology innovators, and regulators, who, darn it, have minds of their own

- A significant occurrence (what one of our clients calls a "digital event") that creates a different landscape—for example, a terrorist attack, a tornado, the collapse of a government, an economic implosion, a major scandal, a product recall, a disruptive technological innovation, or a sizable and viable lawsuit

FIGURE 8-1   Initiative Reporting/Monitoring: A Critical Success Factor for Strategy Implementation

- Necessary shifts in internal priorities
- Project tasks that turn out to be more complex than predicted
- Loss of key resources

During the last few years, many organizations have developed "Balanced Scorecards"[1] of metrics that create a window on a wide vista of performance. We laud executives who look beyond financial metrics, which are the ultimate success meters but which are lagging indicators. However, even those executives who deploy Balanced Scorecards intelligently tend to look at instrument panels that reflect the ongoing operation only in areas such as on-time delivery, customer retention, safety, and employee satisfaction. Rarely do these dashboards provide insights into the return on the increasingly large investment in initiatives.

Effective initiative sponsorship does not require a certain leadership or management style. You may be the type of executive who needs to understand and stay close to operational details. You may occasionally, like Angela in the scenario that opens this chapter, cross the line into micro-management. Or you may be a big-picture person who has no interest in details and relies on others to monitor and manage the tactics. Regardless of how hands-on you are, you should expect progress on key projects to be visible to you and other senior stakeholders.

Even stay-the-course strategies require changes in order to keep up with the dynamics of the market, the competition, regulations, and technology. In our experience, only 30 percent of strategic change results from the incremental improvements that are often referred to as *kaizen*. That puts 70 percent of the change burden on the shoulders of those special projects that we call initiatives. *If initiative performance is not on your instrument panel, you are not monitoring— and therefore not controlling—the effectiveness and pace of strategy implementation.* Your major tactical improvements are also at risk.

Throughout an initiative's life cycle, its results, activities, resource consumption, and pace should be evident. Furthermore, every key project should be reviewed periodically. As with a physical exam, the minimal output of this review is learning that everything is OK. Often, however, it will uncover a need to take action to put a project back on the rails, reinvigorate it, or change its scope or direction.

INITIATIVE REPORTING: PITFALLS TO AVOID

We would be surprised if your organization does no monitoring of project performance. However, you would be typical if you are uncomfortable with its lack of rigor, as reflected by dialogues such as these:

PROJECT SPONSOR: "How is Project A doing?"
PROJECT MANAGER: "Fine."
PROJECT SPONSOR: "Good. Let me know if you run into problems."

PROJECT SPONSOR: "How is Project B doing?"
PROJECT MANAGER: "We're a bit behind, but we'll be back on track before long."
PROJECT SPONSOR: "Good. Let me know how I can help."

PROJECT SPONSOR: "How is Project C doing?"
PROJECT MANAGER: "We're getting there, but it's taking a lot more time and money than we projected."
PROJECT SPONSOR: "What's the length of the delay?"
PROJECT MANAGER: "About six months."
PROJECT SPONSOR: "Wow. How much is the budget overrun?"
PROJECT MANAGER: "I'll have to get back to you on that."

PROJECT SPONSOR: "How is Project D doing?"
PROJECT MANAGER: "It's on hold."
PROJECT SPONSOR: "This is the first time I've heard this. How long has it been on the back burner?"
PROJECT MANAGER: "Three months."
PROJECT SPONSOR: "Why the moratorium?"
PROJECT MANAGER: "It's been eclipsed by other priorities."
PROJECT SPONSOR: "What other priorities?"
PROJECT MANAGER: "I'm not sure."
PROJECT SPONSOR: "Neither am I."

When it comes to Initiative Reporting, executives need to avoid these common pitfalls:

- *Failing to identify the "critical few" metrics.* Some organizations measure everything that moves. They monitor progress, resource consumption, quality, and risk for every activity within every project and for each program. That level of tracking may be useful for project managers and project team members, but executives don't need to see all of it. We have found that every project and program—no matter how complex—has a small number of measures that can provide executives with the information they need to stay on top of strategic initiatives and make decisions regarding changes in direction.

- *Measuring all initiatives as if they were equal.* Acknowledging executives' need for a holistic picture of a program or portfolio, some organizations roll up individual project information into sums and averages. As with other areas of measurement—for example, sales figures that are not broken out by region or manufacturing performance that is not broken out by plant—composites and averages can hide many sins. The overall timing of a cost-containment program may look healthy, but only because two low-priority initiatives that are each 10 percent ahead of schedule inappropriately appear to balance a much higher-priority project that is 20 percent behind.

- *Focusing only internally.* Most reporting is focused on activity and resource consumption against project plans. While this type of information is a critical element of project reporting, on its own it can lead to a dangerous internal focus. For example, every strategic initiative is underpinned by a set of assumptions about the external environment, such as the availability of money at a certain rate, the buying criteria of customers, and the pace of technological change. Over time, reality has a way of coming into conflict with our best-made assumptions. The cost of money may turn out to be significantly higher than predicted. Customers may no longer be willing to pay more for technically superior products. Advances in nanoscience and wireless technology may be more dramatic and rapid than forecasted. Being on plan is great, but not if you are heading blithely for the precipice. Your project and program reporting should also include performance against relevant external metrics, especially those related to customers, shareholders, and regulators.

- *Measuring activities rather than results.* Too much focus on schedule and resource consumption can distract you from the results that the project is achieving. Knowing that a project is on time and within budget is of little comfort if you have no evidence that it is achieving its objectives. Avoid the "we don't know where we're going, but we're making good time" syndrome.

- *Failing to keep it simple.* We have seen reporting processes that require project managers to write extensive monthly summaries of initiative progress. Others employ complex mathematical formulas that attempt to encapsulate the health of a program. If a status-reporting format is onerous, it will fall into disuse or, even worse, contain fabricated information. We've also found that overly labor-intensive tracking and documentation frequently produce status reports that are difficult for executives to interpret. These usually wind up in desk drawers.

- *Failing to maintain the discipline to use the measurement system.* Measuring initiative performance and feeding back the information is nobody's idea of fun. However, without the rigor of regular reporting, your projects are out of control. As a client of ours says, "Getting the reports in is like making people eat their greens; they don't much like it, but they know it's good for them."

THE DIMENSIONS OF PROJECT MONITORING

If your organization has fallen prey to any of these pitfalls, you need to convert the way projects are reported to executives

- From opinion-based to fact-based

- From superficial or mind-numbingly granular to the right level of detail

FIGURE 8-2   The Four Ps of Initiative Success

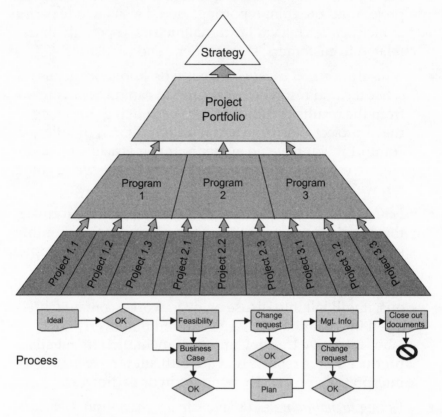

- From containing information that is of value only to a project manager to containing information that is of value to you

- From solely activity-focused to primarily results-focused and, secondarily, activity-focused

To accomplish this objective, we recommend monitoring and controlling the four "Ps" displayed in Figure 8-2:

- *Projects,* or initiatives, are interdependent, nonrepetitive activities directed toward a goal—for example, Project Phoenix, which will rejuvenate the Latin American market; Project Poseidon, which will develop and launch the next generation of underwater digital cameras; and Project Sunlight, which will ensure that company accounting is squeaky-clean.

- *Programs* are sets of projects that share a common goal—for example, your two culture-transformation projects, your three cost-reduction projects, and your four acquisition projects.

- *Portfolio* is the entire waterfront of programs and projects, as described in Chapter 3.

- *Process* is the sequence of activities and protocols through which you identify, approve, plan, staff, implement, and manage projects.

An entire industry has grown up around providing tools and techniques that generate data on every aspect of project health. In shaping what we have found to be the right level and format of information for senior executives, we employ some of these standard techniques and add others that we have developed.

PRINCIPLES OF MONITORING AND CONTROL

We propose three principles for the design of your monitoring and control system:

1. As an executive, you may not need to become immersed in the details of individual initiatives. However, the quality of the intelligence that you receive concerning your primary areas of focus—mission-critical programs, the overall portfolio, and strategy implementation—is only as good as the quality of the information that you receive on individual projects. Individual project status serves as the information foundation on which all subsequent reports will be based (see Figure 8-2). You should pay particular attention to establishing a culture that provides incentives for on-target initiative reporting.

2. If you are given a program summary that is nothing more than a snapshot of current project performance,

your response should be, "Compared to what?" All project and program information should be presented in a "should versus actual" format that highlights the extent of any positive or negative deviations. For example, a "traffic light" reporting format can quickly draw your attention to areas that need attention. At one of our clients, a green light means that actual performance is no less than 90 percent of a plan's goals, yellow signals 80 to 90 percent, and red indicates less than 80 percent.

3.   Where possible, it is valuable to display comparisons of this month/quarter with the previous month/quarter for all key dimensions, enabling you to spot trends.

THE FIVE ELEMENTS OF INITIATIVE REPORTING

Any project, regardless of its scope and nature, can be defined in terms of the results it will yield, the time by which the results will have been achieved, and the maximum investment that will be made to produce those results. We recommend a reporting system that adds two additional factors: issue resolution and stakeholder satisfaction. In the next few pages, we discuss each of these five elements.

RESULTS REPORTING

It is not possible to test whether an initiative has met its objectives until the project assessment that is part of closeout (see Appendix A). However, this assessment focuses on lagging indicators; by the time a project is closed out, the horse is out of the barn. During the project, you will want leading indicators of the likelihood that the expected results will be achieved.

For example, in the mid-1990s, the London Ambulance Service attempted to deploy a computer-aided dispatch (CAD) system that matched emergency calls to ambulance dispatch. The system went live for three days and was then shut down after a massive public outcry, including claims that up to 30 people may have died following its introduction. A public inquiry[2] into this project failure revealed that a principal cause of ambulances arriving too late was that the system had never been adequately tested to see whether it could perform under maximum load.

Some Ambulance Service managers argued that it was not possible to assess capacity until the system went live. However, a strong project manager would not have allowed the system to go live without rigorous testing in a simulated environment. Such testing should have been part of the plan and the measurement of its progress.

New-product introduction projects usually include focus groups or test marketing. IT projects typically involve a pilot project. Executives overseeing business-change projects in which it is not feasible or practical to test solutions formally before their introduction—for example, a culture transformation or a maintenance shutdown—have no less need to assess the likelihood that project activities will ultimately achieve project objectives.

To help make this assessment, we use a measure called Results Performance Index (RPI), which can be calculated using the following process:

1. Review a project's objectives and determine which of them can be delivered before the end of the project.

    Example: *"All relevant staff will be using the system."*

2. Determine which objectives may be partially completed before the end of the project.

    Example: *"All relevant staff will be trained in the use of the new process."*

3. Assess which objectives cannot be measured until some time after the project activities have been completed,

    Example: *"Increase market share"*

4. Weight each objective by assigning it a percentage that reflects its relative contribution to the 100 percent impact of the entire set of objectives.

5. Using the Work Breakdown Structure (see Appendix A), identify the activities that will contribute to the objectives that may be completely or partially accomplished before the end of the project. Estimate the percentage of results to be delivered during each month or another appropriate time interval.

6. As the project progresses, compare the actual delivery of results to the expectations. Produce a score that effectively communicates the "actual" versus the "should."

7. Multiply the score for each objective by its respective weighting. The sum of these weighted scores will produce the RPI.

For example, here is a project statement:

"To develop project management capability within VMB Ltd. by December 31 at a cost not to exceed €70,000."

As displayed in Figure 8-3, the first objective is "focus on high-priority projects," which will be measured in terms of the goal of reducing the size of the portfolio from 120 projects to 30. The project plan indicates that the activities associated with this culling will take place during August and September. The project manager has committed to reducing the portfolio to 60 projects by August 31 and to the target level of 30 by September 30.

The actual performance in August was a reduction in the size of the portfolio to 90 projects. The "Actual versus Should" ratio is 0.5 (reduction by 30 projects rather than 60). A ratio that is less than 1 indicates that performance has fallen short of expectations. Since this objective has a 30 percent relative weighting, its RPI for August is 0.15.

The RPI is calculated for each objective. The sum of the RPIs yields an overall RPI for the initiative. After a bit of orientation to the numbers and format of the Results Perfor-

FIGURE 8-3   A Portion of a Results Performance Index Analysis

Project Statement	To develop project management capability within VMB Ltd. by December 31 at a cost not to exceed €70,000											
Objectives At the end of this project we will have:	Measure	Target at End of Project	Target at 6-Month Post implementation Review	Planned results delivery by month						August actual	Performance Index "Should"	Performance Index "Actual"
				Jun	Jul	Aug	Sep	Oct	Nov			
Focus on high-priority projects	Size of project portfolio	Reduce to top 30	30 projects	120	120	60	30	30	30	90	1	0.5
Weighting for this objective	30%			Weighted performance index							0.3	0.15
Clear roles and responsibilities for all those involved in projects	% of PM competency assessments conducted	80% for those involved with projects	100% for those involved with projects	0%	0%	40%	50%	60%	70%	10%	1	0.25
Weighting for this objective	10%			Weighted performance index							0.1	0.025
Projects delivered on budget	% projects delivered on budget	N/A	100%	20%	20%	20%	20%	20%	20%	20%	1	1
Weighting for this objective	25%			Weighted performance index							0.25	0.25

mance Index, executive overseers find that it helps them answer the key question, "Am I confident that this project will deliver the results that we need?" If the RPI index starts to fall much below 1, those executives should consider whether

- The assumptions on which the project was based have become invalid.

- The plan is flawed and will not deliver the results expected.

- The work is not of sufficient quality to deliver results.

- The quality or quantity of project resources is inadequate.

SCHEDULE AND COST REPORTING

Most organizations measure project progress by examining milestones, which are significant events en route to completion. Examples of milestones are

- Executive approval of the design of new beverage packaging

- Food and Drug Administration confirmation that the clinical trials for a new drug have been successful

- Programmer completion of the coding for the new software

- Operator certification in the new safety procedures

While each step in a plan can be considered a milestone, you do not want to spend your time formally assessing progress as every step in a detailed plan is completed. Furthermore, you don't want the project team to spend more time tracking than doing. For complex plans, the milestones are the major steps on the critical path. For example, the frequently used "stage gates" in a product development process are natural milestones.

Milestone reporting can be useful in giving visibility to project-activity highlights; however, many executives require the more comprehensive measures of project achievement that are provided by earned value analysis. This tool can provide information on project performance in terms of both "time taken" (project schedule) and "investment made" (project cost). It answers these key questions:

- Is this project on schedule?

- Is there enough time left in the schedule to complete the project?

- Where are we against budget?

- Is there enough money left in the budget to complete the project?

- Given the amount of work completed so far, how much money should we have spent?

To provide answers to these questions, earned value analysis uses three principal values:

- *Planned value (or budgeted cost of work scheduled)*, which is the proportion of the overall project time and cost that is planned to be spent from project inception to the reporting date

- *Actual cost*, which is the total cost of doing the work from project inception to the reporting date

- *Earned value (or budgeted cost of work performed)*, which is the proportion of the budgeted time and money that should have been spent for the work that has been done

These values are used to compute variances and indexes, such as

- *Cost Performance Index (CPI)*: The ratio of budgeted to actual costs. CPI = earned value/actual cost.

- *Schedule Performance Index (SPI):* The ratio of work performed to work scheduled. SPI = earned value/planned value.

As an example of the insight that earned value analysis can provide, between January and August, a project team has spent $50,000, which is $5,000 less than expected during this period. Is this good news? No, because the team has spent $16,000 more than was budgeted for the *work* that has been accomplished through August, a CPI of 0.66.

We'll stop before your eyes glaze over. Our goal is not to immerse you in the formulas and the interpretation of the ratios; we merely want to give you confidence that there are tools of varying levels of rigor that, with a bit of education, can be used efficiently by project managers of average capability to produce status information that can keep executives' fingers on the pulse of initiative deployment and strategy implementation.

ISSUE-RESOLUTION REPORTING

The PRINCE2 project management method[3] defines an *issue* as "anything which could have an effect on the project (either detrimental or beneficial)." Project issues can come from anywhere in a project's internal or external environment. The effectiveness with which issues are identified and resolved can have a substantial bearing on the success of a project.

An elaboration of problem-solving, decision-making, and planning tools for issue resolution is beyond the scope of this book; if you want to explore the methods that we use, we recommend that you read *The New Rational Manager*.[4]

From a project-reporting perspective, you want information that tells you whether issues are being quickly recognized and effectively and efficiently resolved. Toward that end, project and program managers need a simple electronic or manual worksheet in which they

• Describe the what, where, when, and magnitude of an issue.

• Outline the method through which the issue will be resolved.

• Name the person who is responsible for resolving the issue and any others who will be involved.

• Indicate the date by which the issue will be resolved.

During a project review, the project or program manager should summarize the number of open issues and the average time for issue resolution. The display suggested in the four bullet points just mentioned should be concise and understandable enough to serve as your double-click on any issues that demand your attention.

Your issues list should not be limited to concerns that are current and undesirable. In organizations in which initiative management is world class, *potential problems and opportunities* are among the issues that are addressed. The "resolution" of these types of issues is viable actions or plans to minimize the probability and seriousness of potential problems and capitalize on opportunities.

On occasion, issues may be so serious or complex that they cannot be resolved within the constraints of the existing project plan. In these situations, the project manager may formally ask to modify the project. You may want to include "unapproved change requests" in your management report.

STAKEHOLDER SATISFACTION REPORTING

A project has a variety of customers: the sponsor, other members of the executive team, the target population, and other affected parties. As a basis for ensuring appropriate stakeholder participation and satisfaction, the opinions of these

FIGURE 8-4   Stakeholder Satisfaction Questionnaire

	1	2	3	4	5
How confident are you that the project objectives will be accomplished? 1 = Not at all confident 5 = Very confident					
Has the business need that the project is addressing changed in importance since the start of the project? 1 = Much less important 3 = Same level of importance 5 = Much more important					
How effectively and efficiently is the project team carrying out this project? 1 = Not at all effectively/efficiently 5 = Very effectively/efficiently					
How well has the project manager/team been communicating project progress and issues to you? 1 = Very poorly 5 = Very well					
Is the nature and amount of your involvement in this project appropriate? 1 = Highly inappropriate (far too much, far too little, or the wrong type) 5 = Very appropriate					

stakeholders should be solicited and tracked. For a strategic initiative, you care about customer perceptions not only of project results, but also of activities, communication, and management. Figure 8-4 shows one organization's monthly questionnaire.

THE INITIATIVE REPORTING PROCESS

For projects that last longer than six months, project managers typically produce a monthly report. For shorter projects, the report is usually weekly. To facilitate this job, we recommend a single, standard reporting template that summarizes performance in each of the five reporting areas just described: results, schedule, cost, issue resolution, and stakeholder satisfaction.

We recommend that a project manager review this report with the sponsor before giving it to the program manager or Program Office for consolidation with other projects in the program. You may or may not want to know the status of an individual initiative, but the information is there if you need it.

PROGRAM REPORTING

A program is a set of projects that share a common goal. Therefore, it follows that a program management report is a consolidation of the constituent project reports. The metrics introduced earlier—RPIs, SPIs, CPIs, issue resolution performance, and stakeholder satisfaction—can be merged to provide a picture of program performance.

However, a simple consolidation may hide some sins because it doesn't reflect the relative importance of a project to the overall program. For example, a pharmaceutical company had a major FDA compliance program. This program had a $40,000 training project with a Schedule Performance Index of 0.8 and a $1,000,000 business-process-redesign project with a Schedule Performance Index of 0.4. Averaging these two values into a *program* SPI of 0.6 would have given the sponsor an inappropriate picture of overall performance.

To get an accurate assessment of the status of a program, we establish the relative importance or "organization value added" (OVA) of each project. The performance of projects that are expected to deliver higher OVA should have a greater influence in the assessment of overall program performance. This objective can be accomplished by assigning each project a simple relative weight—a "Portfolio Evaluation Score"—that can be calculated during the portfolio priority-setting process described in Chapter 3.

Figure 8-5 displays a monthly report for a small but strategically important program of human resource improvement projects. The performance of each project, described in the "Individual Project Status" section, uses the five reporting dimensions we have outlined. The projects are sorted in order of the Portfolio Evaluation Score to ensure that the most important projects are reviewed first. In the "Program Summary" section, you will see that the organization value-added scores have been used to produce weighted results, schedule, and cost indexes that provide a balanced view of overall program performance.

FIGURE 8-5 Sample Program Status Report

Individual Project Status

Portfolio Evaluation Score	Project Name	Current Phase Until:	Project Sponsor	Project Manager	Project Status — This Month	Project Status — Last Month	Open Issues	Issue Resolution Time (days)	Unapproved Change Request	Results (RPI) — This Month	Results (RPI) — Last Month	Schedule (SPI) — This Month	Schedule (SPI) — Last Month	Cost (CPI) — This Month	Cost (CPI) — Last Month	Stakeholder Satisfaction — This Month	Stakeholder Satisfaction — Last Month	RPI × Portfolio Evaluation Score	SPI × Portfolio Evaluation Score	CPI × Portfolio Evaluation Score
238	Employee Journey (Career Planning)	Execution Dec 03	Sarah	Fiona	OK	Caution	2	15		0.82	0.80	0.77	0.75	1.10	0.99	5	5	195	183	261.8
204	Kronos	Definition Mar 03	Leslie	Sally																
188	Diversity Action Team	Execution Nov 03	Nicky	Lucy	Caution	Caution	3	20	9	0.75	0.62	0.69	0.60	0.65	0.67	5	3	141	130	122.2
175	Management System	Execution June 04	Leslie	Sally	OK	Critical	10	41		0.80	0.67	0.81	0.75	1.20	0.98	4	4	140	142	210
																	Totals	476	455	594

Program Summary

Portfolio Evaluation Score	Project Name	Current Phase Until:	Program Sponsor	Program Manager	Program Status — This Month	Program Status — Last Month	Open Issues	Issue Resolution Time (days)	Unapproved Change Request	Results (RPI OVA / PES) — This Month	Results (RPI OVA / PES) — Last Month	Schedule (SPI OVA / PES) — This Month	Schedule (SPI OVA / PES) — Last Month	Cost (CPI OVA / PES) — This Month	Cost (CPI OVA / PES) — Last Month	Stakeholder Satisfaction — This Month	Stakeholder Satisfaction — Last Month	RPI × PES	SPI × PES	CPI × PES
805	HR Improvement Program	Execution June 04	Simon	Sam	Critical	Critical	15	25	1	0.592	0.527	0.565	0.525	0.738	0.662	4	4	476.2	454.7	594

PORTFOLIO REPORTING

There are two basic questions to be answered at the portfolio reporting level: "Are we doing the right things?" and "Are we doing things right?" The "doing things right" dimension can be assessed through a management report that rolls up the program reports (see Figure 8-5) into a snapshot of all of the programs in the portfolio. It displays the relative performance of each program within the portfolio and enables an interested party to double-click on any program to see the status of individual projects.

Regarding "doing the right things," your business strategy should contain a set of key indicators of strategic success. This set of metrics usually includes overall financial results, performance of key products and markets, performance against competitors, and customer satisfaction.[5] These measures should enable you to determine whether the portfolio is on the right strategic track.

PROCESS CONTROL

The final reporting dimension is process performance. Rather than focusing on the status of individual projects and programs, this domain is concerned with the strength of the pylons that support all projects and programs. There are two areas in which you should exercise some level of control: the quality of decisions being made as projects move through their life cycle and the degree to which project and program management processes are working.

THE "PROJECT PASSPORT": A TOOL FOR OPTIMIZING PROJECT DECISION MAKING

Your project management process (see Chapter 7) should include a means for capturing the information needed to set expectations and support decision making throughout the life of an initiative. To this end, traditional project management methodologies use a variety of control documents, such as

- *Project initiation forms* that capture the initial intent

- *Charters* that make the business case for projects and serve as approval documents

- *Project management plans* that capture the detailed "who," "when," and "how much"

- *Monthly reports* that summarize project progress and issues throughout implementation

- *Stage-gate reports and checklists* that ensure all elements of work in one stage have been completed satisfactorily before moving onto the next stage

- *Change requests* that solicit approval for any significant modifications to projects during their implementation

- *Closeout reports* that capture lessons learned and compare the results to the promises

Many people believe that this amount of documentation is necessary to provide adequate project-portfolio visibility and control. However, for all but the most complex projects, we have found that it is difficult to get project managers to use these documents effectively. And, we doubt that you, as an executive sponsor, would sit still for this volume of reporting. While most formal project management methodologies demand significant levels of process control (for example, PRINCE2 has 26 control documents), our experience suggests that less is more.

The need to simplify initiative documentation led to our development of a tool that we call a *Project Passport*. The passport is a single document that accompanies a project and gets "stamped" as it travels through its life cycle. Specific information is added to the passport as the project evolves. For example, at the end of the project definition phase, the passport may contain basic information on the project's purpose and scope. By the time the project reaches the end of the planning phase, the passport may contain business-case information as well as a detailed plan and risk analysis.

A Project Passport focuses your project community on collecting only the information that you need to make effective decisions. We have found that a passport has these additional benefits:

- It takes less time to prepare documentation, freeing up resources to produce deliverables.

- Project information is easily accessible because it is all in one place.

- It eliminates confusion about which document to use at which time.

- Training people in the use of one document is more effective and efficient than training them to use several.

For a typical initiative, the passport includes answers to the questions in Figure 8-6.

ARE YOUR PROJECT AND PROGRAM MANAGEMENT PROCESSES WORKING?

You may be in the enviable position of sponsoring initiatives that routinely accomplish their objectives without significantly overrunning their budgets and schedules. However, initiatives may achieve what appears to be success by compromising ongoing operations. Or milestones may be met only if project team members work around the clock seven days a week, which turns these valued people into zombies. If so, your projects sit on a rocky foundation. Without a robust and well-maintained initiative management process

- There will be no common approach to the way people define, plan, and implement projects. ("If we're on the same project, why aren't we on the same page?")

- There will be no framework around which knowledge and experience can be gathered and used for subsequent projects. ("Haven't we messed up this kind of project before?")

- There will be insufficient clarity concerning people's individual roles and responsibilities. ("I'm a sponsor; what am I supposed to do?")

- You will not be able to produce consistently high-quality project- and program-status information. ("Where are we?")

FIGURE 8-6   A Project Passport Template

Life-Cycle Phase	Information to Be Added to the Passport at Each Stage
Initiation	Why is the change necessary?
	What is the proposed scope of this project?
	What if we do nothing?
	What alternatives have been looked at?
	What will be the key objectives for this project?
	What is out of scope?
	Who is the sponsor for this project?
	Who are the key stakeholders?
	What are the principal risks to success?
Definition	What specific benefits will this project deliver?
	How will this project contribute to our goals?
	What budget and resources will be required?
	What assumptions and constraints should be considered?
	What dependencies or interfaces should be considered?
	What are the major project deliverables and milestones?
	Who will manage this project?
Planning	How will all the work be scheduled?
	Who will be responsible for each work package?
	How will identified risks be managed?
Implementation	How are we progressing against our schedule?
	How are we doing against budget and resource requirements?
	What issues do we face?
	What new risks have been identified?
	What changes do we need to make to the plan?
Closure	Have we completed our hand-over to the users?
	Have we closed the project and communicated where needed?
	Have we captured useful knowledge and lessons learned?
	Have we evaluated the results that we have achieved?

- You will be forced to rely on individual heroics, which, while noble, are not a recipe for long-term success. ("What will we do if Charlie gets hit by a bus?")

The second area of project control ensures that your initiative and program management processes deliver the results that you expect. You can accomplish this objective by installing a control process that mirrors the one that most likely underpins your core line processes, such as order fulfillment and product development. That process should embody these simple analysis and control principles, which you may recognize as the backbone of Six Sigma:

- *Define.* Identify the critical few activities that are most pivotal to the success of each project management subprocess. For example, in project definition, these might be project scoping, objective setting, and financial appraisal.

- *Measure.* You will want to measure your project management process using objective criteria (e.g., financial appraisal conformance to a template, plan sign-off cycle time). You may also want to measure stakeholder perceptions.

- *Analyze.* Plot the performance score on a control chart that displays upper and lower control limits, facilitating the identification of "common causes" and "special causes" of performance deviations.[6]

- *Improve.* Get to the root of special causes and take corrective action.

- *Control.* To ensure that special causes stay eliminated and to reduce process variation, we recommend that you direct your project management process owner to (1) continuously refine the process design, (2) put the skills and systems in place to ensure first-class execution, and (3) institutionalize the five reporting dimensions outlined earlier.

COMMENT

If you are like most senior executives, you invest a significant amount of your people's time in generating—and a significant amount of your own time in reviewing—information on the previous period's financials, customer-satisfaction ratings, quality performance, and/or productivity levels. Valuable as these numbers are, they do not provide you with direct insight into the rate at which the business is evolving to meet new challenges. Since projects are the vehicles that execute strategy, we believe that your project, program, portfolio, and process measurement and reporting should be as rigorous and disciplined as your monitoring and control of operational performance.

NOTES

1. R. Kaplan and D. Norton, *The Balanced Scorecard: Translating Strategy into Action* (Boston: Harvard Business School Press, 1996).

2. Brian Randell, "Report of the Inquiry into the London Ambulance Service. London: South West Thames Regional Health Authority, 1993." ftp://cs.ucl.ac.uk/acwf/info/lascase0.9.pdf

3. Colin Bentley, *Practical PRINCE2* (London: The Stationery Office, 1998).

4. Charles Kepner and Benjamin Tregoe, *The New Rational Manager* (Princeton, N.J.: Princeton Research Press, 1981).

5. Mike Freedman with Benjamin Tregoe, *The Art and Discipline of Strategic Leadership* (New York: McGraw-Hill, 2003).

6. John Bicheno, *QUALITY 50: A Guide to Gurus, Tools, Wastes, Techniques and Systems* (Buckingham, U.K.: Picsie Books, 1994).

CHAPTER 9

WORLD-CLASS STRATEGY IMPLEMENTATION

*P*HILIP BORDEN, THE HAMMERSMITH INDUSTRIES *CEO introduced in Chapter 1, is frustrated with the snail's pace of
strategy implementation. He understands that the remedy is
not simply pushing his people harder. He has come to appreciate the
adage on a poster that has become a staple of cubicle decor: "However much you want something to work, it's not going to do what
it's not designed to do." Hammersmith, like many businesses, is
structured to run day-to-day operations, and it does that well.
However, the processes, roles, and culture needed for initiative
excellence have never been baked into the enterprise. It is time to
preheat the oven.*

*Philip's executive team is astute enough to understand that there
is no magic elixir that will transform Hammersmith's ability to execute strategic initiatives. So, the executives are resisting the tempta-
tion to simply dip everyone in project management workshops,
create and staff a project office, or install an off-the-shelf project management process. They realize that they will establish the right balance between functional and initiative responsibilities only by
adapting each enterprise performance variable—leadership, business*

processes, measurement, skills, information systems, structure, culture, and issue resolution—to Hammersmith's unique circumstances.

The executives' first action was to capture the projects and programs that were already underway or planned. Armed with an understanding of the current project landscape, they set out to make the tough decisions about the size and nature of their project portfolio. But, as they began their deliberations, another question emerged: Was the Hammersmith strategy clear enough to provide the rudder for their change program? Their conclusion: "Probably not."

To start Hammersmith on the road to implementation excellence

1. The leadership team formulated a strategic vision. The team members clarified and documented product scope and emphasis, market scope and emphasis, sources of growth, and competitive advantages. As the debates got more frequent and heated, they disproved an assumption that they had had before the meeting: that they all had the same strategic vision and merely needed to document it.

2. Philip overcame his understandable aversion to creating new positions and appointed a strategy implementation officer (SIO). This new member of the top team—a hard charger who had formerly headed up marketing—was given responsibility for creating and maintaining the project portfolio and for introducing the systems, processes, and capabilities needed to manage it. The position became one of the most exciting and value-added jobs in the company.

With strategy as the bus and the SIO as the driver, Hammersmith is set to embark, identifying, setting priorities on, and deploying the initiatives that will fuel its journey to strategy implementation. The company is prepared to go through the steps in each of the seven areas outlined in this book.

An executive has two responsibilities: formulating strategy and implementing that strategy. This book has focused on the latter. We have learned that strategies—even those that keep an organization on the same path or reflect a patently obvious new way to succeed in the future—do not spontaneously take root as a result of their unimpeachable logic.

Your processes for business development, supply-chain management, customer support, and billing/collection, as well as your back-office processes such as budgeting, hiring, and information systems management, may be exemplary. If these processes are well-oiled machines, the quality of your products, services, and customer relationships is ensured. Efficiency is institutionalized. Money is intelligently managed.

However, if this book has one goal, it is to highlight the fact that these processes are only half of the success equation. If your initiative infrastructure is weak (see Figure 9-1), you will not be able to execute your strategy.

WHERE SHOULD YOU START?

Based on your exploration of the executive role in initiative success, you may, like Hammersmith's Philip Borden, see a need to substantially or incrementally improve your initiative support processes, structure, and environment. This journey, which is likely to spawn—you guessed it—one or more projects, begins with two questions:

1.   What are your initiative execution needs?
2.   Where should you start?

To develop a pinpointed answer to the first question, we suggest that you complete the brief self-assessment in Appendix B. If you run into some "I don't knows," you may need an independent initiative audit.

You may have identified deficiencies in many or all of the seven areas depicted in Figure 9-1. However, you probably do not have the bandwidth to close all of the gaps at once.

Do you have a project-portfolio management process, fronted by an identification protocol that ensures that all

FIGURE 9-1   The Seven Critical Success Factors for Strategy Implementation

potentially valuable initiatives are in the hopper? If not, that is probably where you will want to begin. After providing a baseline of your current project capacity and activity, that process will guarantee that your strategy is driving your future initiative load and priorities.

To help assign priorities to your needs (the unchecked boxes in Appendix B), we suggest these criteria:

• Maximize long-term positive impact on initiative success.

• Maximize short-term positive impact on initiative success.

- Minimize negative impact on ongoing operations (the nonproject dimension of your business).
- Minimize implementation time.
- Minimize implementation cost.

After applying these criteria, you may find that your most pressing priority is addressing some cultural issues. Or you may identify the need for a common methodology as the first domino that needs to fall. Or you may need to make some structural changes.

COMMENT

Initiatives may be a highly visible or a largely hidden dimension of your performance landscape. In either case, they represent both opportunities and threats. On the one hand, they are the means of growing your business, accomplishing nonstandard work, and improving transactional processes. On the other hand, they can be a resource sinkhole.

To wrestle with both the upside and the downside of projects, executives cannot sit on the sidelines. You must play a pivotal role in addressing each of the seven success factors that anchor this book. If you question the value of investing your precious time in improving your organization's project execution, please remember:

Initiatives are the vehicles that deliver your strategy. While others need to make key contributions, only you can drive. What's at stake is nothing less than the realization of your vision for the future success of your organization.

AN INITIATIVE MANAGEMENT PROCESS

C HAPTER 7 OUTLINES THE BENEFITS of installing an Initiative Management process that is standard across functions and types of projects. As Figure A-1 shows, the quality of the process and the discipline with which it is used make it one of the seven factors that influence the effectiveness and efficiency of strategy implementation. This appendix outlines a process that has been used successfully in all sectors, organization sizes, cultures, and continents.

The process depicted in Figure A-2 strikes a balance between robustness and user-friendliness. For project managers, a double- or triple-click on the steps reveals tools, protocols, and guidelines; we've spared you that level of granularity. Throughout the explanation of this process, "you" refers to the appropriate person in your organization rather than to you as an individual.

This process conforms to the Project Management Body of Knowledge (PMBOK),[1] which is the de facto standard for approaches and tools in this arena.

The running example we present in this appendix is the simple highlights of a strategic initiative. This methodology

FIGURE A-1   Initiative Management Process: A Critical Success Factor for Strategy Implementation

has been used for highly complex projects, such as enterprisewide information system installations, multimillion-dollar product launches, new market entries, and plant closures.

PROJECT DEFINITION

STEP 1A: STATE THE PROJECT

It is essential that you begin a project with a concise articulation of the project goal, the completion deadline, and the maximum cost. This project statement forces a common understanding of project scope, project depth, and resource commit-

FIGURE A-2   A Project Management Methodology

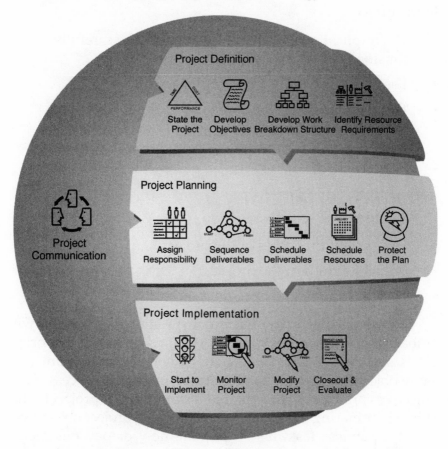

ment. Time spent getting this statement right pays significant dividends by facilitating up-front communication and serving as the touchstone throughout the project. While others may provide input, this statement is the responsibility of the project sponsor. For example, here's the project statement for a strategic initiative:

Launch the company rebranding by September 30 at a cost not to exceed $400,000.

The project statement may change as the project evolves. However, because substantive changes in this statement reflect modifications to the direction of and/or the investment in the project,

- The implications of each change should be carefully considered.

- The sponsor must approve the changes.

- The changes should be conveyed to the project team, the target population, and anyone else to whom the original project statement was communicated.

STEP 1B: DEVELOP OBJECTIVES

Project objectives specify

- The specific outcomes of the project

- The aspirations of the project

- The constraints that limit the project

Objectives answer two seminal questions: "Why are we embarking on this project?" and "What will tell us if this project is successful?" Ensuring that all stakeholders share the same objectives is a critical ingredient in project success. The objectives provide the beacon that illuminates the project path. While hammering out a set of five to fifteen project objectives is not a painless task, it's a "pay me now or pay me later" proposition. Failure to establish objectives up front is likely to result in confusion, aggravation, and miscalibration later. As with the project statement, the sponsor owns the objectives. For the rebranding project statement in Step 1a, the objectives may include these expected outcomes:

- *Define a brand that reflects the new company strategy.*

- *Establish internal understanding of the what, why, and how of the rebranding.*

- *Ensure that all products and promotional materials embody the new brand.*

- *Communicate the new brand to our target markets.*

and these aspirations (each of which can and should be measured):

- *Be top-of-mind in our niche.*
- *Become one of the most recognized and respected brands in the country.*
- *Generate new orders as a direct result of the launch.*

and these constraints:

- *Ready in time for the October trade show*
- *No more than $200,000 in out-of-pocket expense (e.g., to our marketing advisory firm)*
- *Not slow down the release of the X-32 upgrade*

STEP 1C: DEVELOP WORK BREAKDOWN STRUCTURE

In this step, you specify the deliverables that need to be produced and the activities that need to be carried out during the project. You begin by forging consensus on the macro "buckets of work." You then decompose these buckets into increasingly greater levels of detail until you reach the level at which activities can be assigned to individuals or teams. As a partial example for the rebranding initiative introduced in the earlier steps,

1. *Brand "essence" defined*
2. *Tag line and graphic designed*
3. *Brand essence and rationale communicated internally*
4. *Brand essence and rationale communicated externally*
5. *Packaging changed*
6. *Brochures and Web site updated*

A full Work Breakdown Structure typically has substeps (1.1, 1.2, 1.3 and perhaps 1.1.1, 1.1.2, 1.1.3). Many formats, tools, and software programs can be used to document this display of the tasks to be completed.

FIGURE A-3   Step 1d: Identify Resource Requirements

Step	Out-of-Pocket Financial Resources	Internal Human Resources	Equipment/ Facilities/Materials Resources
6. Brochures and Web site updated	$35,000: Marketing advice $15,000: Printing $25,000: Web design	*Professional:* 25 person-days *Administrative:* 6 person-days	None

The project statement is the "what" of the project. The objectives are the "why." The Work Breakdown Structure is the "how."

STEP 1D: IDENTIFY RESOURCE REQUIREMENTS

In this step, you specify the internal and external resources—financial, human, equipment, facilities, and materials and supplies—that will be needed to accomplish each of the elements in the Work Breakdown Structure. An example is given in Figure A-3.

Various estimating tools and processes are available to facilitate this step.

PROJECT PLANNING

STEP 2A: ASSIGN RESPONSIBILITY

In this step, you add the "who" dimension, including

- Those who have the skills, knowledge, information, and experience to carry out the tasks in the Work Breakdown Structure

- Those who will provide the resources

- Those who must support, approve, or commit to each task

To make certain that everyone knows who is taking the lead, you highlight the individual with the primary responsibility for each activity. Figure A-4 gives an example.

FIGURE A-4   Step 2a: Assign Responsibility

Work Breakdown Element	Executive Team	VP Marketing	Market Analyst	Customer Council
1.1 Strategic positioning developed	Define positioning	Provide input	Provide market and competitive analysis	Provide feedback
1.2 Brand characteristics identified	Approve	Develop & recommend		Provide input
1.3 Concise statement of brand identity created	Approve	Analyze & recommend	Generate alternative statements and pluses and minuses of each	Approve

More detailed activities could be entered in each box; however, that detail is usually put in the next level of the Work Breakdown Structure. For example, "1.1 Strategic positioning developed" may decompose into

1.1.1   *Mission statement created*

1.1.2   *Future product scope and segmentation defined*

1.1.3   *Future market scope and segmentation defined*

1.1.4   *Future competitive landscape projected*

1.1.5   *Future competitive advantages identified*

During this step, you evaluate other individual and departmental demands to ensure that neither this project nor other work suffers.

STEP 2B: SEQUENCE DELIVERABLES
The Work Breakdown Structure displays *what* needs to be done, but not *when* it should be done. It would have been premature for you to identify the timing before assigning responsibility. When sequencing deliverables, you determine and display:

FIGURE A-5   Step 2b: Sequence Deliverables

Work Breakdown Element	Completion Time	Precedence Relationships
1. Brand "essence" defined	3 days (as part of overall strategy formulation)	None
2. Tag line written and graphics designed	1 day	After Step 1
3. Brand essence and rationale communicated internally	30 days	After Step 2

- The activities that need to precede others

- The activities that should be carried out in parallel

- The elapsed and lag time of each activity

- The critical path into which other activities feed

Figure A-5 continues our example.

The word *deliverable* and the *"-ed"* format of the Work Breakdown elements help to give the user and the evaluator an output focus.

In many projects, a network diagram is constructed at this point. This graphic provides a visual display of the sequence of activities. It is usually helpful to highlight the "critical path" of mission-critical steps.

STEP 2C: SCHEDULE DELIVERABLES

During this step, you add the dates to the sequence. The project start and end dates and all of the steps accomplished earlier are inputs to this step.

For most projects, a Gantt chart or some other graphic display facilitates the display of start and stop dates for each activity. An example is shown in Figure A-6.

STEP 2D: SCHEDULE RESOURCES

You have identified the resources. You have set the dates. Now you need to match the two. The output of this step is individuals with dates for specific activities blocked on their

FIGURE A-6 Step 2c: Schedule Deliverables

ID	Task Name
0	To develop recruitment, induction, and training processes
1	1.1 Recruitment plan and process built
2	1.1.1 Recruitment plan for all functions developed
9	1.1.2 Individual roles defined and agreed upon
12	1.1.3 Detailed recruitment plan and budget agreed upon
19	1.1.4 Ongoing recruitment process developed
23	2.1 Induction process installed
31	3.1 Training plans and process developed
32	3.1.1 TNA interviews completed
37	3.1.2 Training plan defined and agreed upon
41	3.1.3 Training vendors identified and selected
42	3.1.4 Core training delivery begins
43	3.1.5 Training process installed

Timeline columns: March (02/18, 02/25, 03/04, 03/11, 03/18, 03/25), April (04/01, 04/08, 04/15)

173

calendars. You may do the scheduling solely with the individuals or with the participation of their managers. You evaluate the overall demands on individuals to ensure that they are not over- or underutilized and make adjustments accordingly. If designated individuals have become unavailable, you make decisions regarding replacement, outsourcing, or changes to the project schedule.

STEP 2E: PROTECT THE PLAN
Your plan may be the result of rigorously applying the eight steps just outlined. It may reflect input from all of the right people. You may have experience with this type of project. However, your plan is not invincible. Even superbly constructed buildings should be insured. Once the plan is complete, but before implementation begins, you need to answer the following questions, which form the core of a process called Potential Problem Analysis[2]:

- What could compromise the performance, timing, or cost of this project? (Potential Problems)

- What could bring about these Potential Problems? (Likely Causes)

- What can we do to make it less likely that these Potential Problems will occur? (Preventive Actions)

- What will we have ready to minimize the damage if they do occur? (Contingent Actions)

- What will tell us to activate the Contingent Actions? (Triggers)

An example is given in Figure A-7.
You don't want to focus solely on the negatives. In addition to minimizing the risk, you want to maximize the benefit by answering these Potential Opportunity Analysis[3] questions:

- What additional benefits could be reaped from this project? In other words, what objectives other than those listed in Step 1b could be achieved? (Potential Opportunities)

FIGURE A-7   Step 2e: Protect the Plan

Potential Problem	Likely Cause	Preventive Action	Contingent Action	Contingent Action Trigger
Executive team cannot reach consensus on brand characteristics	√ Failure to understand the objective of the exercise √ Differing views on the most powerful characteristics	√ Have marketing firm educate the team before the discussion √ Use a facilitator to guide the consensus building	CEO will consider all opinions and decide on the characteristics	Consensus not achieved by Day 3 of the strategy offsite

- What is likely to create these opportunities? (Likely Causes)

- What can we do to make it more likely that these opportunities will present themselves? (Promoting Actions)

- What will we have ready to enable us to maximize the benefit if the opportunities do arise? (Capitalizing Actions)

- What will tell us that the opportunity is knocking? (Triggers)

An example is given in Figure A-8.

The Potential Problem and Potential Opportunity Analyses typically cause you to add to or change the steps in the plan. The Work Breakdown Structure is modified so that it includes taking the Preventive and Promoting Actions and readying the Contingent and Capitalizing Actions. These actions may also necessitate adjusting the dates. For example, the Contingent Action cited above requires brand-focused marketing initiatives to be put on hold until the characteristics decision is made.

PROJECT IMPLEMENTATION

STEP 3A: START TO IMPLEMENT

You clarify roles and administrative requirements. You establish ground rules for working together and with stakeholders.

FIGURE A-8   Step 2e: Protect the Plan (continued)

Potential Opportunity	Likely Cause	Promoting Action	Capitalizing Action	Capitalizing Action Trigger
Rebranding strengthens relationships with current A-tier customers	Involvement of the Customer Council in the rebranding process	Formally build council participation into the process (while respecting their time)	Account managers schedule appointments to identify needs we are not currently meeting and propose products to meet those needs	Formal and informal feedback from A-tier customers indicates a greater appreciation for our products and the services that support them

You develop protocols for monitoring and resolving issues. The project is officially launched.

STEP 3B: MONITOR PROJECT

During this step, the project manager and other participants keep an eye on project performance, schedule, and expense. At any given point, the project team and other interested parties should know where the project stands. In this step, the project manager is not merely recording and reporting on progress; she or he is looking for and acting on current and potential problems and opportunities. Chapter 8 is dedicated to management reporting.

STEP 3C: MODIFY PROJECT

Even a well-defined and well-planned project may need to be modified. The sponsor may change jobs. Resources may become unavailable. Other projects may be deemed to have higher priority. Unforeseen events (internal or external) may occur. Project success is not measured by how closely the implementation follows the original plan; it is measured by the achievement of the objectives on time and on budget. To hit these targets, you may have to modify the project a number of times en route.

STEP 3D: CLOSE OUT AND EVALUATE

Once a project has achieved its objectives, you will be tempted to put it behind you and move on to the next challenge. Too many projects fade away rather than officially end. You need to communicate project completion, wrap up financial and administrative details, debrief, provide feedback, document learnings, and celebrate success.

The "lessons learned" dimension of closeout is particularly important and all too often overlooked. You want to capture and disseminate anything that can benefit future projects. During the Close Out and Evaluate step, you should answer these questions:

- Do all stakeholders—especially the target population and other "customers" of the project—agree that the objectives have been achieved?

- Did the project come in on time? If not, why not?

- Did the project stay within budget? If not, why not?

- Did the sponsor and the project manager play the appropriate roles?

- Did the project team members make the expected contributions?

- How well did the project team members work together?

- How effective and efficient was the communication—up, down, and sideways—during the project?

- What did you learn about this type of project?

- What did you learn about implementing projects of any kind in this environment?

- What capabilities were created during this project? How can we leverage those capabilities to accomplish our strategic objectives?

PROJECT COMMUNICATION

As Figure A-2 shows, "project communication" should be built into each step in each phase. Some communication can be done via documents; some requires person-to-person interaction. These meetings—which may be formal or informal, remote or face-to-face—may include some or all of the following: sponsor, project team members, the target population, other stakeholders, subject-matter experts, and those with experience in this type of project. The purposes of this step are to ensure that everyone is on the same page, to identify and address glitches and potential problems, and to keep the game plan current.

Accurate, understandable, timely communication is a critical dimension of strategy implementation. It can compensate for shortcomings in many of the steps outlined in this appendix.

BUILDING *YOUR* PROJECT MANAGEMENT PROCESS

If your people use this generic project management framework intelligently, you will see significant improvements in their ability to define, plan, and implement projects. However, this change in individual behavior may not be enough to deliver the organization-wide improvement you need in order to implement your strategy. The tools will need to be used within the context of a business process that defines and installs the right levels of project decision making, visibility, and control. Toward that end, we recommend the following approach:

1. *Identify the priority areas for installing a project management process.* Your project portfolio (See Chapter 3) will help you determine the type of work you need to do to institutionalize initiative management. For example, if your portfolio contains "one-off" projects, such as closing a business or building a capability, a simple process based on the "define/plan/implement" methodology, overlaid with the necessary controls, will suffice. However, project species that recur—like product development/commercialization, marketing campaign design/deployment, and information systems design/installation—benefit from the development of replicable stages.

2. *Agree on the Project Management tool kit.* You want your
    project teams not only to use a common process, such as
    that outlined in this appendix, but to use common tools
    within each step in the process. For example, you want a
    consistent format for "Develop Work Breakdown Struc-
    ture" (Step 1c) and "Assign Responsibility" (Step 2a).
    Adopting a best-practices toolkit will ensure (1) smooth
    cross-project and cross-functional communication and (2)
    rapid understanding and intelligent questioning from the
    executives to whom project status reports are presented.

3. *Define future processes.* At this point, you need to deter-
    mine the stages for each species of *recurring* project that
    you identified in the first step. Replicable stages will
    facilitate the project reporting and control that we dis-
    cuss in Chapter 8. For example, these types of projects
    may have these life-cycle stages:

Marketing projects
  - Idea validation
  - Concept design
  - Concept development
  - Program launch

Product development projects
  - Market evaluation
  - Financial evaluation
  - Product build and test
  - Product release

Software projects
  - Systems analysis and design
  - Solution design and build
  - Solution testing
  - Acceptance and sign-off

These are just the headlines. Robust processes—such
as the Stage-gate protocol for new-product development[4]
exist for a number of types of recurring projects. Successful deployment requires customizing these standard
processes for your organization.

In large projects, each stage in the life cycle may benefit from being treated as a project unto itself. The model in Figure A-9, developed for one of our pharmaceutical clients, shows how (1) a project is born (see Chapter 2) and positioned (see Chapter 3) through an initiation step, (2) project stages proceed through the definition—planning—implementation process, and (3) projects are closed out.

4.   Plan and implement process introduction. During this final step, your executive team, with extensive input from others, creates a comprehensive plan for implementing each of the new project management processes. This plan includes not only the introduction of the new processes and control documentation, but also the changes that need to be made to policies, resources, information systems, job designs, skills, and reward systems. Regardless of the nature and extent of the change, a key output of the plan is communicating the "what," "why," and "how" to all stakeholders.

FIGURE A-9   Executing Multistage Projects

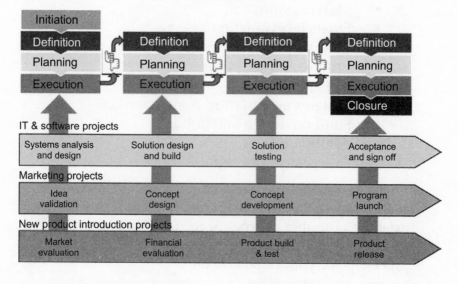

NOTES

1. Project Management Institute Publications, *A Guide to the Project Management Body of Knowledge: 2000 Edition*, 2001

2. Charles Kepner and Benjamin Tregoe, *The New Rational Manager* (Princeton, N.J.: Princeton Research Press, 1997), pp. 139–166.

3. Ibid.

4. Robert G. Cooper, *Winning at New Products: Accelerating the Process from Idea to Launch*, 3rd ed. (New York: Perseus Publishing, 2001).

B

DIAGNOSING
YOUR INITIATIVE
EXECUTION

O ESTABLISH THE BASIS FOR SELECTING and setting priorities for the diet and exercise components of your strategy implementation "wellness program," we suggest that you take a comprehensive physical exam. The purpose of this appendix is to use the framework presented in this book to (1) diagnose your strategy implementation performance, (2) identify the cause(s) of any deficiencies, and (3) direct you to the place in the book that provides ideas, examples, and tools that should help you remove those deficiencies.

The questions that follow are designed to help you identify

- Areas of strength

- Areas in which you do not perform well consistently

- Areas that you are not addressing at all

- Areas that are not current weaknesses, but are at risk

DO OUR PROJECT RESULTS MEET MY EXPECTATIONS?

❑ We have not done an exemplary job of implementing our strategy.

❑ I am frequently disappointed in the results of strategic initiatives.

❑ Even if they achieve the intended objectives, strategic and tactical projects frequently come in late and/or over budget.

❑ We are inconsistent. Certain types of initiatives (e.g., acquisitions and product launches) tend to go well, but others (e.g., marketing programs and recruiting initiatives) do not.

❑ I am less in control of our initiative work than of our day-to-day operations.

❑ I don't know the cause(s) of the deficiencies in our project performance.

If you checked any of these boxes, please troubleshoot your initiative deployment by responding to the following questions. They deal with all of the strategy implementation success factors that anchor this book and appear in Figure B-1.

DO WE INITIATE THE PROJECTS THAT WE NEED?

❑ We launch the initiatives that enable us to effectively and efficiently implement our strategy.

❑ We use projects as the engines for substantial operational improvement.

❑ Our resource-intensive initiatives are commissioned because of the needs of the business rather than being rooted in ego, power, or the negotiating skill of the initiator.

❑ Projects are officially launched, as opposed to "just happening."

FIGURE B-1   Critical Success Factors for Strategy Implementation

☐ The approval process does not discourage people from proposing worthwhile initiatives.

If any of these boxes are unchecked, you should benefit from the ideas and tools in Chapter 2.

DO WE HAVE THE RIGHT QUANTITY AND MIX OF PROJECTS IN OUR PORTFOLIO?

☐ We have a manageable number and scope of initiatives.

❑   We know our project capacity (i.e., how many person-hours per month we can dedicate to special projects without compromising ongoing operations).

❑   Strategic initiatives and lower-impact projects get the resources—including executive attention—that they deserve.

❑   Our project priorities change when necessary, but not too often.

❑   We have the discipline and attention span to stick with needed initiatives (rather than abandoning them in favor of sexy new projects and campaigns to "get back to the basics" of daily operations).

❑   When an initiative no longer makes sense, we kill it rather than allowing it to grind to completion.

❑   The executive team regularly takes stock of our project portfolio, using criteria derived from the strategy to ensure that we're working on the right things.

If any of these boxes are unchecked, you should benefit from the ideas and tools in Chapter 3.

DOES OUR ORGANIZATION STRUCTURE SUPPORT OPTIMUM INITIATIVE EXECUTION?

❑   We have a central clearinghouse ("initiative central") for project monitoring, control, and reporting.

❑   We have assigned an appropriate owner of the process through which projects are generated, defined, priori-tized, scheduled, staffed, deployed, monitored, and closed out.

❑   Someone is responsible for "connecting the dots" among related projects (e.g., ensuring that the marketing initia-tive is in concert with the order-fulfillment initiative).

❑   A person or group is responsible for identifying and bringing to the surface cross-project conflicts (e.g., two

projects making impossible demands on a single
resource or one project optimizing in a way that causes
another to suboptimize).

❑   A person or group is responsible for providing the executive team with a holistic picture of overall project-
portfolio performance (the "helicopter view" of the
entire initiative waterfront).

❑   Someone is responsible for taking the temperature of the
"initiative culture" and reporting any deficiencies to
those who can overcome them.

❑   A person or group is responsible for documenting and
archiving project lessons learned.

❑   We have not allowed our Project Office to devolve into a
bureaucratic policing function that impedes, rather than
supports, optimum initiative performance.

If any of these boxes are unchecked, you should benefit
from the ideas and tools in Chapter 4.

DO WE HAVE AN INITIATIVE-FRIENDLY CULTURE?

❑   People at all levels see strategic initiatives as the engines
for propelling us forward rather than as distractions
from the real business of making products and serving
customers.

❑   If a project achieves its objectives on time and within
budget, there are positive consequences for the sponsor,
the project manager, and team members. If a project fails
to achieve its intent or exceeds its planned resources,
there are negative consequences.

❑   Talented people seek out opportunities to contribute to
initiatives (as sponsors, project managers, and team
members).

❑   People get frequent, pinpointed, balanced feedback on
their performance on initiatives. Projects are adequately

factored into our performance appraisal system and our informal day-to-day feedback.

❏ Being assigned as a project manager or team member is generally perceived as a vote of confidence. Project managers are respected as current or potential leaders.

❏ We give project contributors the skills they need to carry out their roles.

❏ We have a culture that fosters "skunk works" projects (unsanctioned, low-visibility initiatives pursued—often on personal time—by true believers).

If any of these boxes are unchecked, you should benefit from the ideas and tools in Chapter 5.

DO WE ESTABLISH APPROPRIATE PROJECT ROLES?

❏ Executives play the appropriate initiative sponsor role.

❏ We staff projects with "the best and the brightest," as opposed to people whose removal from day-to-day operations has minimal impact.

❏ Project managers fully understand the roles that they should and should not be playing.

❏ Project team members understand the roles that they should and should not be playing.

❏ When asked about an initiative, members of the target population (those intended to be affected by project results) usually (1) know that it is underway, (2) understand its purpose, (3) can define what it means to them, and (4) think it will have a positive impact.

❏ When people are not assigned full-time to projects, we take action to make sure that they are able to do justice to both their project and their nonproject responsibilities. We ensure that workload imbalances do not cause either initiatives or ongoing operations to suffer.

If any of these boxes are unchecked, you should benefit from the ideas and tools in Chapter 6.

DO WE HAVE A ROBUST, PRACTICAL INITIATIVE MANAGEMENT METHODOLOGY?

❑ We have developed or adopted a process through which projects are defined, planned, implemented, and closed out.

❑ Our Initiative Management process is robust enough to address the needs of complex projects, but simple enough to be understood and used by project contributors at all levels.

❑ We do a good job executing our Initiative Management process.

❑ We make good use of project management software.

❑ We have an organization-wide common approach and common language for project management.

❑ Projects begin with a game plan, as opposed to careening headlong into action. We don't confuse activity with productivity.

❑ Our Work Breakdown Structures (activity and deliverable definitions) are at the right level (not too general to guide projects or too detailed to be practical).

❑ We give projects—particularly strategic initiatives—the funding that they need if they are to achieve the expected results.

❑ Initiatives are not frequently thrown off course by external or internal events or circumstances that should have been anticipated.

❑ We learn from our projects. For example, each time we develop a product or install an IT system, we draw on the lessons from previous initiatives of this type.

❑   Initiatives are not bogged down by too many or overly
     lengthy meetings.

     If any of these boxes are unchecked, you should benefit
from the ideas and tools in Chapter 7 and Appendix A.

DO WE EFFECTIVELY AND EFFICIENTLY MONITOR
AND REPORT ON INITIATIVE PERFORMANCE?

❑   I and my colleagues on the executive team know how
     many projects are underway and how much of our
     human and financial resources they are consuming.

❑   The executive team is sufficiently close to initiative
     progress. Project status information is readily available.

❑   We know, early on, if projects are failing to achieve their
     objectives or are coming in late and over budget.

❑   Project status reporting focuses on giving executives the
     facts that they need in order to make midcourse correc-
     tions rather than on complaining, anatomy protection,
     and blame fixing.

❑   Project status reporting is efficient.

     If any of these boxes are unchecked, you should benefit
from the ideas and tools in Chapter 8.

DO OTHERS SEE YOUR SITUATION THE SAME WAY?

You will benefit from knowing whether your perceptions in
these areas are aligned with those of other executives and of
the nonexecutives who serve as project managers and team
members or are frequently part of the target population. This
checklist is a vehicle for determining the degree of calibration.
If only some people highlight a weakness, they should provide examples for the illumination of the others.

Index

ABOUT THE AUTHORS

Alan Brache, Executive Director, Business Solutions at Kepner-Tregoe, Inc., has been a consultant and executive for over 25 years. A noted authority on business strategy and implementation, Brache is the author of two groundbreaking books: the best-selling *Improving Performance: How to Manage the White Space on the Organization Chart* and the critically acclaimed *How Organizations Work: Taking a Holistic Approach to Enterprise Health.*

Sam Bodley-Scott is Vice President at Kepner-Tregoe, Inc. His experience helping numerous international organizations implement change initiatives has led directly to the development of many of the concepts and tools presented in this book. Bodley-Scott created and managed Kepner-Tregoe's European Strategic Project Management consulting practice, enabling clients to implement strategy successfully through a combination of change and program management solutions.